HSK 4 CHINESE GRAMMAR 中文...

- A COMPLETE REFERENCE FOR YOUR SUCCESS V2021 HSK 汉语语法

HSK (NEW SINCE 2009) 新汉语水平考试

Contents

About the Author:

David Yao, the founder of www.LegooMandarin.com and Educational Video Courses Online (www.Edeo.biz), born in china, resides in Kuala Lumpur, Malaysia, holding Master degree from University Malaya, has 25 years' experience in mandarin teaching for foreigners, creating a SYSTEM (more than 200 mandarin courses) designed for foreigners to study Chinese as secondary language. He practices Tai Chi for almost 30 years and establishes Tai Chi Fitness Organization (http://taichifitness.org/) to modernize and promote Tai Chi for fitness and health.

Scan QR code for Lifetime Access to Full Video course together with this book

@ the best price in Udemy:

Our Story

"Share with You What We Know Best" is our Slogan. We start with LEGOO Mandarin and now expand the system into other topics: Bahasa Malaysia, IT eCommerce, Accounting and Finance, Tai Chi Fitness and Qi Gong. You can learn anytime anywhere!

In addition to be a **Contents Provider**, we also provide **Online Systems,** which can be easily integrated with your school or company online system or use separately. We are using Udemy and other more than 10 similar platforms for video courses marketing. The Amazon KDP, Google Books and Apple iBooks are platforms we publishing our textbooks in addition to our own platform. We provide consultancy service to save your time and give you the best tips on how to leverage your efforts using all these amazing platforms. Please contact us for quotations (very reasonable price).

We can assign our trained teachers to conduct **live lesson** through Webinar, Skype and YouTube, Facebook at reasonable price.

Licencing Program to schools & Resellers

We offer Licencing Program to schools! More schools are using our system! You can use quiz, video course, PPT and PDF under our Licencing Program. Customized course development with your own LOGO can be done. Please contact us for details and quotations (very reasonable price).

Licencing Program to Resellers

We offer Licencing Program to Resellers, book stores and other Platforms (Websites, Google stores, Groupons, Facebook stores). We provide contents such PDF books, online Quiz and Video Courses. You can list our contents in your platform. We will share on 50-50 sales basis. We can provide technical assistance to integrate our contents with your system and help response within 24 hours.

Please contact us by whatsapp +60163863716.

David Yao Amazon Kindle Author Central page

For Hardcopy or paperback books at best price with reduced postage, please visit: David Yao Amazon Kindle Author Central page:

http://bit.ly/david-amazon-kdp (USA)

https://www.amazon.co.uk/-/e/B07PR3LTMQ (UK)

https://www.amazon.de/-/e/B07PR3LTMQ (German)

http://www.amazon.fr/-/e/B07PR3LTMQ (France)

https://www.amazon.co.jp/~/e/B07PR3LTMQ (Japan)

https://www.amazon.com/-/e/B07PR3LTMQ (USA)

Preview and download books by David YAO at Apple Book Store:

https://books.apple.com/us/author/david-yao/id584331956

Our Video Courses in Udemy

For Audio and more detailed explanations, please refer to our Video course platform at:

https://www.udemy.com/user/legoomandarindavidyao/

Preface 1: No Grammar in Chinese Language?

Grammar is a borrowed concept from western language. There is no Grammar in Chinese in certain senses. The greatest truths are the simplest! In simple way, Chinese Grammar is just the sequence construction of Characters, like our LEGOO brand

In the complicated way, Chinese Grammar can drive you to crazy! In this book, I will show you the simplest truths in my own way, if not academic way!

I start from basic grammar by referring to the syllabus or Curriculum of following Chinese Exams:

Edexcel GCSE / IGCSE Chinese (4CN, 5CN03F, 5CN03H),

Edexcel A1 A2 (GCE, A Level) Chinese,

Cambridge IGCSE Chinese (0523, 0547),

AQA GCSE Chinese (AQA-46702F, AQA-46702H)

IB Chinese B (SL, HL) (Second Language)

IB Chinese A (SL, HL) (First Language)

SAT Chinese,

AP Chinese

HSK (Chinese Proficiency Test),

YCT (Youth Chinese Test)

Then I started from the basic Chinese Grammar, then gradually to the advance levels. I try to present Grammars in the most logic way and give all the sample Chinese sentences the best possible English Translation.

In this book, I will arrange Chinese Grammar into following main topics:

Part 1 Brief Introduction

Part 2 Grammar about Phrases, classified into Noun, Verb, Adjective, Pronouns etc. 11 categories.

Part 3 Grammar about Sentence Structure

Part 4 Grammar about Grouping Sentences

The first book was printed in 2011 and many students call it "LIFE SAVING" for their exam. The book give a quick revision for the coming GCSE Chinese, IGCSE Chinese, IB Chinese, SAT Chinese, HSK (Chinese Proficiency Test), YCT (Youth Chinese Test) exam! Grab it.

The 2019 edition can be used with our Chinese Vocabulary Books and our Online Video Courses. It takes our years' painful effort to edit and please respect our copy rights. Thanks for your support for us to creating better contents for you!

The 2021 version added more sentences to illustrate the grammar concept and the usage. This whole series adjusted accordingly for IGCSE, IB Chinese etc.

David YAO, Founder of www.LegooMandarin.com and www.edeo.biz

March 27, 2019

(November 10, 2020 Finalized the Version 2020)

Preface 2

We have vocabulary series for New HSK. There are total 9000 vocabularies with the possible Best English Translation for your better understanding with our many years' experience in HSK and GCSE teaching. We also give HSK level classifications which will give you a cross reference for your Chinese standard. The vocabularies are classified into following 12 categories then ranked according HSK levels.

1 名词　　　míngcí　　　Noun

2 动词	dòngcí	Verb
3 形容词	xíngróngcí	Adjective
4 代词	dàicí	Pronouns
5 数词	shù cí	Numeral
6 量词	liàngcí	Classifier; Measure Word (MW)
7 副词	fùcí	Adverb
8 连词	liáncí	Conjunction
9 介词	jiècí	Preposition
10 助词	zhùcí	Particle
11 叹词	tàn cí	Interjection
12 象声词	xiàngshēngcí	onomatopoeia

Many students call it "LIFE SAVING" for their exam. The book give a quick revision for your coming exam! Grab it! Thanks for your support for us creating better contents for you! It takes our years' painful effort to edit and please respect our copy rights.

How to use this book effectively?

Tips:

1. Tally the words you DON'T know in front. This will shorten your Vocabulary. If you tally a work 4 times. This means this word bullies you FOUR times. Then? Remember or Kill it!

2 For students who take Cambridge IGCSE Chinese (CIE 0523, 0547) HSK 5, the HSK Classifications will give you cross reference. If your level are IB HL (HSK 6), all HSK 6 words you need to know the meaning and reading, HSK 5 and lower words you should know how to write out. This will help you to highlight the priorities of your study. That's why many students call it "LIFE SAVING" for their exam.

What's new in Version 2020?

Add similar words to compare the meaning or usage:

Verb + Object (Things, Sth.)

喝水 h ē shu ǐ   Drink water

把 + Object (Things) + Verb (Have Sth. done)

把水喝了   b ǎ shu ǐ h ē le   Drink water

打开书   d ǎ k ā i sh ū   Open the book

把书打开   b ǎ sh ū d ǎ k ā i Open the book

吃饭　　　　　chīfàn　　　　　　　　　Eat meal (eat food)

把饭吃了。　bǎ fàn chī le.　　　　　　Have the meal eaten.

吃完饭　　　Chī wán fàn　　　　　　Finish meal

把 + Object (Things) + Verb + Complementary (which shows the result of action)

把饭吃完　bǎ fàn chī wán　　　Have the meal finished (Finish the meal!)

把饭吃干净　　　bǎ fàn chī gānjìng　　　　　Eat all cleanly.

Compare with another Passive words 被 (by)

Object (Things, Sth.) + 被 +（Sb.）+ Verb　(Sth. Done by Sb.)

饭被他吃了。　　fàn bèi tā chī le.　　　　The meal was eaten by him.

饭被他吃完了。　Fàn bèi tā chī wán liǎo. The meal was eaten all by him.

饭被他吃干净。　Fàn bèi tā chī gānjìng. The meal was eaten cleanly by him.

Add similar words to compare the meaning or usage:

…点钟　　…diǎn zhōng　(名)… O'clock

一点钟　　Yī diǎn zhōng (名) one o'Clock　HSK 1　new

两点钟　　Liǎng diǎn zhōng　(名) two o'clock　HSK 1　new

Comparing with 小时

小时　xiǎoshí　(名) hour HSK 2　new

半小时　　bàn xiǎoshí　half an hour.

两个小时　liǎng gè xiǎoshí　two hours

一天有 24 个小时。　yītiān yǒu Èrshísì gè xiǎoshí.　There are twenty-four hours in a day

Fine difference highlighted!

得　　dé　　(动) get; gain; obtain:　HSK 4　new

得到 dédào　　(动) get; obtain; gain; receive

得　　děi　(动) must; have to:

More illustrations:

顿　dùn (量) (used for number of times of scold, meal, persuade)　HSK 4 new

三顿饭	s ā n d ù n f à n	three meals.
挨了一顿骂	ā ile y ī d ù n m à	get a scolding
饱餐一顿	b ǎ oc ā n y ī d ù n	have a big meal; eat and drink one's fill
一顿美餐	y ī d ù n m ě ic ā n	a delicious meal
一顿臭骂	y ī d ù n ch ò um à	A scolding

The new HSK (Chinese Proficiency Test) Introduction:

The new HSK (Chinese Proficiency Test) is an international standardized exam that tests and rates Chinese language proficiency. It assesses non-native Chinese speakers' abilities in using the Chinese language in their daily, academic and professional lives. HSK consists of six levels, namely the HSK (level I), HSK (level II), HSK (level III), HSK (level IV), HSK (level V), and HSK (level VI).

II. Test Levels

New HSK	Vocabulary
HSK (Level I)	150
HSK (Level II)	300
HSK (Level III)	600
HSK (Level IV)	1200
HSK (Level V)	2500

HSK (Level VI)   Over 5,000

1. Test takers who are able to pass the HSK (Level I) can understand and use very simple Chinese words and phrases, meet basic needs for communication and possess the ability to further their Chinese language studies.

2. Test takers who are able to pass the HSK (Level II) have an excellent grasp of basic Chinese and can communicate in simple and routine tasks requiring a simple and direct exchange of information on familiar and routine matters.

3. Test takers who are able to pass the HSK (Level III) can communicate in Chinese at a basic level in their daily, academic and professional lives. They can manage most communication in Chinese when travelling in China.

4. Test takers who are able to pass the HSK (Level IV) can converse in Chinese on a wide range of topics and are able to communicate fluently with native Chinese speakers.

5. Test takers who are able to pass the HSK (Level V) can read Chinese newspapers and magazines, enjoy Chinese films and plays, and give a full-length speech in Chinese.

6. Test takers who are able to pass the HSK (Level VI) can easily comprehend written and spoken information in Chinese and can effectively express themselves in Chinese, both orally and on paper.

The levels of the new HSK correspond to the levels of the Chinese Language Proficiency Scales for Speakers of Other Languages (CLPS) and the Common European Framework of Reference for Languages (CEF), GCSE, IGCSE, AS, A Level (A1, A2), IB, SAT, AP as follows:

New HSK	Vocabulary	CLPS	CEF	GCSE/IGCSE	AS, A Level (A1, A2)	IB (SL)	IB (HL)	SAT	AP
HSK (Level VI)	Over 5,000	Level V	C2				5000		
HSK (Level V)	2500		C1		2500	2500	2500	2500	2500
HSK (Level IV)	1200	Level IV	B2	1200	1200	1200	1200	1200	1200
HSK (Level III)	600	Level III	B1	600	600	600	600	600	600
HSK (Level II)	300	Level II	A2	300	300	300	300	300	300
HSK (Level I)	150	Level I	A1	150	150	150	150	150	150

The HSK (Level V) assesses test takers' abilities in the application of everyday Chinese. It is the counterpart of the Level V of the Chinese Language Proficiency Scales for Speakers of Other Languages and the C1 Level of the Common European Framework of Reference (CEF). Test takers who are able to pass the HSK (Level V) can read Chinese newspapers and magazines, enjoy Chinese films and plays and give a full-length speech in Chinese.

1. Test Target

The HSK (Level V) is intended for students who have studied Chinese 2-4 class hours per week for more than two academic years. These students have mastered 2,500 commonly used words and related grammar patterns.

II. Test Content

The HSK (Level V) test is made up of listening comprehension, reading comprehension and writing sections and contains a total of 100 items.

Section			Number of Items		Duration (Min)
I. Listening		Part I	20	45	About 30
		Part II	25		
Filling out the answer sheet(Mark your answers for listening comprehension on Answer Sheet)					5
II. Reading		Part I	15	45	45
		Part II	10		
		Part III	20		
III. Writing		Part I	8	10	40
		Part II	2		
Total		/	100		About 120

The test will last for 125 minutes in total (including 5 minutes in which the test takers fill in personal information).

1 代词　dàicí　Pronoun

1.1 人称代词 rénchēng dàicí Personal Pronouns

我　　wǒ　　(代) I, me　HSK 1　new

你　　nǐ　　(代) you [second person singular]:　　HSK 1　new

他　　tā　　(代) he; him　HSK 1　new

她　　tā　　(代) she; her　HSK 1　new

们　　　　　men　1 [used after a personal noun or a noun to show plural number]:

我们　　　　wǒmen　　　　we

你们　　　　nǐmen　　　　you (plural)

孩子们　　　háizimen　　　the children.

人们　　　　rén men　　　people (plural)

们　　　　　men　2 [is not used when the pronoun or noun is preceded by a numeral or an intensifier:]

三个教师们　　sān gè jiàoshīmen　　　three teachers

很多姑娘们　　hěnduō gūniángmen　　　many girls

我们　　　　wǒmen　　　(代) we; us　HSK 1　new

你们　　　　nǐmen　　　(代) you (plural)

他们　　　tāmen　　　(代) they [indicating the male sex, or male and female together]

她们　　　tāmen　　　(代) [indicating the female sex] they

您　　　　nín　　　　(代) (敬) you (respect way)　　HSK 2　new

它　　　　tā　　　　　(代) [neuter gender] it　　HSK 2　new

它们　　　tāmen　　　(代) they

大家　　　dàjiā　　　(代) all; everybody　　HSK 2　new

大家来想办法　　dàjiā lái xiǎng bànfǎ　　Let's put our heads together. (Everyone come to think of a way)

自己　　　zìjǐ　　　　(代) oneself:　　　HSK 3　new

你自己　　nǐ zìjǐ　　　yourself

我自己　　wǒ zìjǐ　　　myself

他们自己　tāmen zìjǐ　they themselves

哥哥自己　gēgē zìjǐ　　my brother himself

自己的事自己做。　　zìjǐ de shì zìjǐ zuò.　　your own thing do yourself

我弟弟会自己穿衣服。wǒ dìdì huì zìjǐ chuān yīfú.　My younger brother can dress himself.

别人　　　　biérén　　　（名）other people; others; people :　　HSK 3　new

别人想法不同　　biérén xiǎngfǎ bùtóng　　Other people think differently.

自己做的事，为什么要拉¹上别人？　zìjǐ zuò de shì, wèishéme yào lā shàng biérén?　　Why drag in others when it was all your own doing?

自己做错了，不能赖²别人　　zìjǐ zuò cuòle, bùnéng lài biérén　You should not blame others for what is your own fault.

打击别人，抬高³自己　dǎjí biérén, tái gāo zìjǐ　　attack others so as to build oneself up

俩　　　　liǎ　　　　（代）（口）two (of people)　　　HSK 4　new

咱俩　　　zán liǎ　　　we two; the two of us

俩＿＿＿＿＿＿＿＿＿liǎ　2 some; several:

¹拉　　lā　　7 drag in; implicate:

²赖　　lài　　4 blame sb. wrongly; put the blame on sb. else:

³抬高　tái gāo（动）raise; heighten; enhance:

就这么俩人？　　　jiù zhème liǎ rén?　Just these few people?

他们俩形影不离。　　tāmen liǎ xíngyǐngbùlí.　They are always together

他们俩一见钟情[4]。　　tāmen liǎ yījiànzhōngqíng　They two fell in love at first sight

他们俩是父子关系。　tāmen liǎ shì fùzǐ guānxì.　They two are father and son

他们俩　　　tāmen liǎ　（代）the two of them

他人　　tārén　（代）another person; other people; others

不要取笑他人的失误　bùyào qǔxiào tārén de shīwù　Don't laugh at others' mistakes

等　　děng （代）and so on; etc.:　HSK 4 new

等　　děng　4 [used after a personal pronoun or a noun to indicate plural number]:

老李等三人　　lǎo lǐ děng sān rén　Lao Li and two others.

我等五人　　wǒ děng wǔ rén　the five of us

[4]钟情　zhōngqíng　be deeply in love with

等   děng   5   and so on; etc.:

等等   děng děng   and so on; and so on and so forth; etc.

梨、苹果、葡萄等   lí, píngguǒ, pútáo děng   pears, apples, grapes and so on

等   děng   6 [used to end an enumeration] : such as

北京、上海、广州等大城市   běijīng, shànghǎi, guǎngzhōu děng dà chéngshìBig cities such as Beijing, Shanghai, and Guangzhou

各   gè   (代) each; every: HSK 4   new

各位先生女士   gèwèi xiānshēng nǚshì   Ladies and gentlemen .

各国   gèguó   each country.

各…各…   gè…gè…   1 each . . . his own . . .

各走各的路   gè zǒu gè de lù   each goes his own way

各…各…   gè…gè…   2 all kinds of:

各行各业   gè háng gè yè   all walks of life; all trades and professions

各式各样   gè shì gè yàng   (形) of various kinds

在谈判桌上，双方各说各的观点。   At the table, each side state their own points of view.

这些小公司现在都各有各的特点。 These small companies now have their own discrete identity.

据说这次拳击比赛，各有各的绝招，胜负难分。 It's said that in this bout both boxers have their strengths, so it's hard to know who will win.

公司即将倒闭，对今后的出路员工们各有各的打算。 The company will close down. Regarding the future, each employee has his or her own plan. on their own papers. No one cheated.

其次　　　qícì　　(代)(副) next; secondly; then:　HSK 4　new

质量是主要的，数量还在其次. Quality is primary while quantity is of secondary importance.

想学好外语，首先要多听，其次要多说。 To learn a foreign language well, one should first listen to it more; and secondly speak it more.

首先要重视内容还要注意文风 Pay attention first of all to the content, and then the style　V2020

我买东西，首先考虑质量，其次才考虑价格。 When I go shopping, my first concern is the quality, then the price.

我还不想走——首先，我没有准备好，其次，正在下雨。 I don't want to go yet - in the first place I'm not ready, and in the second place it's raining.

奶酪是我最喜欢的食品，其次是巧克力。　　　　Cheese is my favourite food and, next to that, chocolate. (= Cheese is the only food that I like more than chocolate.)

任何　　　　　　　　rènhé　　　　（代）any; whatever　HSK 4　new

没有任何希望　　　There isn't any hope.

他没有任何理由不去　　He has no reason whatsoever not to go.

任何事情都是有利有弊的，所以让人有时候很难取舍。　　　　Everything has both advantages and disadvantages, and therefore sometimes it's hard to make a choice.

所有　　　　　suǒyǒu　　（代）all; what you have　　HSK 4　new

把所有的劲儿都使出来　　　exert all one's strength　　V2020

咱们　　　　zánmen　　　　　（代）we [including both the speaker and the person or persons spoken to]　　HSK 4　new

你来得正好, 咱们一起议一议 You've come in the nick of time. Let's put our heads together

咱们先喂饱孩子，然后再吃饭吧。 Let's feed the kids first and have our dinner after.

快一点儿，咱们赶快出发吧，否则就来不及了。 Come on, let's get this show on the road or we'll be late.

咱们先赶紧吃点东西吧。 Let's just grab a quick bite.

咱们别争了。 Let's not (UK also don't let's) argue.

今天下午咱们去游泳吧。 Let's go swimming this afternoon.

另外 lìngwài (代) in addition; moreover; besides; other; another HSK 4 new

但是到这时事情有了另外的一面。 But by now there was another side to the tale.

另外，为满足爱吃甜食的人的口味，这家小餐馆还提供多种甜点。 And to satisfy your sweet tooth, this café has desserts galore.

你觉得搬到另外一座城市去怎么样？ How would you feel about moving to a different city?

我们不会让另外的那个候选人轻易获胜的。 We're going to give the other candidate a run for her money.

一群孩子正在学校操场上嘲弄推搡另外一个孩子。 A group of children were goading (= laughing at or pushing) another child in the school playground.

她又给我看了另外一组照片，这次是孩子们玩耍的情景。　　　She showed me another group of pictures, this time of children playing.

我觉得我能得到那份工作，但另外那个候选人有经验方面的优势。

I thought I would get the job, but the other person who was being considered for it had experience on his side.

最近已有将近3000人失去了工作，另外还有3000人也面临着失业的危险。
Almost 3,000 jobs have been lost recently, and a further 3,000 are on the line.

如果你的行李超重，还得另外再付钱。　　If your luggage is overweight, you have to pay extra.

某	mǒu	(代) certain; some:	HSK 5 new
某人	mǒu rén	a certain person .	V2020
某日	mǒu rì	at a certain date	V2020
在某种程度上	zài mǒu zhǒng chéngdù shàng	to some (or a certain) extent	
在某种意义上	zài mǒu zhǒng yìyì shàngln a sense		

| 某某 | mǒu mǒu | (代) so-and-so | |

某某大夫　　mǒu mǒu dàfū　　Dr. so-and-so; a certain doctor.

某某学校　　mǒu mǒu xuéxiào　a certain school

巴结某人　　bājié mǒu rén　　try to win sb's favour

某某夫妇　　mǒu mǒu fūfù　　Madame So-and-so

她总会把最新的小道消息及时告诉我——你知道吗，路那头的某某人怀上了孩子，某某人刚买了汽车。　　　　She always keeps me up to date with the latest gossip - you know, so-and-so from down the road is having a baby and so-and-so's just bought a car.

彼此　　　　bǐcǐ　(代) each other; one another　　HSK 5　new

这两个人只是彼此听说过。　　　　The two men know each other only by reputation.

这些日子我们从未碰面——我们彼此的圈子不同。　　　　We never meet these days - we move in different circles (= do not have the same group of friends).

恋爱中的男女必须为彼此挤出些时间。　　In a relationship you have to make time for each other.

他们坐在桌子的两端，彼此互不搭理。　　They sat at opposite ends of the table (to/from each other), refusing to talk.

他们彼此变得非常友好。　　They've become very pally (with each other).

他们两个已经在一起共事 5 年多了，彼此都有一点儿厌倦。   They had been working together for over five years and they had both become a little stale.

在一起两年后，我们意识到彼此不适合对方，决定各走各的路。 After a couple of years together, we realized we weren't really happy and decided to go our separate ways.

他们对彼此的爱与日俱增。   It came to pass that their love for each other grew and grew.

各自   gèzì   (代) each; respective: HSK 5 new

既要各自努力，也要彼此帮助   This calls for both individual effort and mutual help.

如何   rúhé   (代) how; what :   HSK 5 new

不管结果如何   whatever the results.

你觉得这本小说如何?   How do you like this novel?

他不知如何是好   He didn't know what to do.

明天能不能去长城那要看天气如何。   It depends on the weather whether we can go to the Great Wall tomorrow.

其余   qíyú   (代) the rest; the remainder: HSK 5 new

其余的人跟我来　The others come with me.

其余的都是妇女　All the rest are women.

1.2 指示代词　Zhǐshì dàicí　Demonstrative pronoun

这儿　zhè'er　　　(代) here; now; then:　　HSK 1　new

这儿　zhè'er　　　(代) here; now; then:　　HSK 1　new

这里　zhèlǐ　　　(代) here　　HSK 1　new

那　　nà　　　(代) that　　HSK 1　new

那儿　nà'er　　　(代) there; that place　　HSK 1　new

那里　nàlǐ　　　(代) there; that place　　HSK 1　new

我对这儿很满意，虽然没有花园，但是离河边很近，　Wǒ duì zhè'er hěn mǎnyì, suīrán méiyǒu huāyuán, dànshì lí hé biān hěn jìn,　I am very satisfied here, although there is no garden, but very close to the river,

那里有草地，有大树，还有鸟；　　nà li yǒu cǎodì, yǒu dà shù, hái yǒu niǎo; There is lawn, there are trees, there are birds also;

那里有三个苹果。　　　Nà li yǒusān gè píngguǒ. There have three apples. (Lit.) There are three apples.

他在那里。 Tā zài nàlǐ.　　　　He　at　there. (Lit.)　　　He is there.

每　　měi　　　　(代) every; each:　HSK 2　new

这么　zhème　　　(代) so such; this way; like this:　　　V2020

外面下雪了, 难怪这么冷　　　　No wonder it's so cold. It's snowing.

你的脸色这么难看, 不是病了吧?　　　You don't look well. Are you ill?

其他　　　　qítā　　(代) other; else:　HSK 3　new

还有其他事吗?　hái yǒu qítā shì ma?　　Anything else?

其他人就不用去了　　　Qítā rén jiù bùyòng qùle　Others needn't go

1.3　疑问代词　　　Yíwèn dàicí　　Interrogative pronouns
谁　　shuí　　　(代) who:　HSK 1　new

你找谁?　nǐ zhǎo shuí?　　Who are you looking for?

谁　　　shuí　　　（代）2 nobody:

谁都不知道他　　shuí dōu bù zhīdào tā　　Nobody knows him.

谁　　　shuí　　　（代）3 anybody:

有谁愿意跟我们一起去？　　yǒu shuí yuànyì gēn wǒmen yīqǐ qù?　Would anyone like to go with us?

谁的　　　Shuí de　　　（代）Whose

谁买的书？Shuí mǎi de shū?　Who bought the book?

哪　　　nǎ　　（代）which; what:　HSK 1　new

哪儿　　nǎ'er　（代）where; wherever:　　HSK 1　new

哪里　　nǎlǐ　（代）where; wherever:　　HSK 1　new

哪　　　nǎ　　（代）1 which; what:　　HSK 1　new

你想借哪本书？　nǐ xiǎng jiè nǎ běn shū?　Which book do you want to borrow?

他是哪国人　　Tā shì nǎ guórén　What country is he from?

你最喜欢哪种颜色？　nǐ zuì xǐhuān nǎ zhǒng yánsè?　What is your fa vourite colour?

你哪天有时间？　Nǐ nǎ tiān yǒu shíjiān?　When (or which day) are you free?

哪　　　nǎ　　　2 any　HSK 3　new

你借哪本书都可以　　　　nǐ jiè nǎ běn shū dōu kěyǐ You can borrow any book you like.

这两种颜色我哪种都不喜欢　zhè liǎng zhǒng yánsè wǒ nǎ zhǒng dōu bù xǐhuān I like neither of the colours.

哪天都行　nǎ tiān dū xíng　Any day will do.

哪　　　　　nǎ　　　　　3 (副) [used in a rhetorical question]:

哪有你这样对待老人的？　nǎ yǒu nǐ zhèyàng duìdài lǎorén de? How could you treat old people like this?　HSK 5　new

没有他的帮助你哪能有今天？Méiyǒu tā de bāngzhù nǐ nǎ néng yǒu jīntiān? How could you possibly be what you are today without his help?

哪个　　　nǎge　　　　　(代) 1 which; which one:

哪个公司？nǎge gōngsī?　　Which company?

你要哪个？Nǐ yào nǎge?　Which one do you want?

哪个　　　Nǎge　　　　　(代) 2 who:

哪个？　nǎge?　　　　Who is it?

哪里　　　nǎlǐ　　　　　(代) where; wherever:

你在哪里住？　nǐ zài nǎlǐ zhù?　Where do you live?

你住在哪里？　　　nǐ zhù zài nǎlǐ？　Where do you live?

在哪里工作都一样　　Zài nǎlǐ gōngzuò dōu yīyàng　It doesn't make any difference where I work.

哪里　　　nǎlǐ　（代）[used to form a rhetorical question] : How could I… HSK 5 new

我哪里知道他已经走了 wǒ nǎlǐ zhīdào tā yǐjīng zǒuliǎo How could I know he had left already?

他哪里会说汉语，不过认识几个字罢了　tā nǎlǐ huì shuō hànyǔ, bùguò rènshí jǐ gè zì bàle　He doesn 't really speak Chinese. He only knows a few characters

你的帮助太大了-- 哪里，哪里　　nǐ de bāngzhù tài dàle-- nǎlǐ, nǎlǐ　　You have given us a lot of help --- It is nothing

哪里 nǎlǐ　　　（代）where, not at all. (where got, where got), a polite way reply to praise to you by others. HSK 5 new

你这篇文章写得真好！哪里, 哪里！ Nǐ zhè piān wénzhāng xiě dé zhēn hǎo! Nǎlǐ, nǎlǐ!　The article you wrote is really nice! Not at all

什么 shénme　　（代）[used to indicate interrogation] what　HSK 1 new

你说什么？　　　nǐ shuō shénme?　What did you say? or Beg your pardon?

什么 shénme　　（代）2 [used to indicate sth. indefinite]:　　HSK 2 new

我饿了，想吃点什么。 wǒ èle, xiǎng chī diǎn shénme.　I am hungry. I feel like having a bite

我们好像在什么地方见过　　Wǒmen hǎoxiàng zài shénme dìfāng jiànguò It seems that we've met somewhere before.

什么　shénme　　（代）3 [used before 也 or 都 to indicate the absence of exceptions within the stated scope] :　HSK 3 new

他什么也不怕。　tā shénme yě bùpà He is afraid of nothing.

什么　shénme　　（代）4 [in a phrase or sentence with one 什么 preceding another，the 1st 什么 always determines the meaning of the 2nd 什么]:

有什么就说什么　yǒu shé me jiù shuō shénme　　speak freely; say all you have got to say.

你喜欢什么就拿什么。　nǐ xǐhuān shénme jiù ná shénme　　You can take whatever you like.

什么　shénme　　（代）5 [used to indicate surprise or displeasure]:　HSK 4 new

他是什么人？　tā shì shénme rén? What sort of person is he?

什么　Shénme　　（代）6 [used after a verb to indicate reproach or disapproval] HSK 4 new

急什么，时间还早呢?　jí shénme, shíjiān hái zǎo ne?　What's the hurry? It's still early.

什么　Shénme　　（代）7 [used before parallel words or phrases to indicate enumeration]:　HSK 5 new

什么乒乓球啊，羽毛球啊，篮球啊，排球啊，他都会。 shénme pīngpāng qiú a, yǔmáoqiú a, lánqiú a, páiqiú a, tā dūhuì He can play table tennis, badminton, basketball, volleyball, and what not.

什么的 shénme de (代) and so on; and what not: HSK 6 new

下班后，他总喜欢到酒吧间喝杯啤酒什么的。 xiàbān hòu, tā zǒng xǐhuān dào jiǔbā jiān hē bēi píjiǔ shénme de. After work, he likes to go to the bar for a mug of beer or something like that

这有什么，我不过做了我应该做的事吧了！ zhè yǒu shé me, wǒ bùguò zuòle wǒ yīnggāi zuò de shì bale I have only done what I ought to. That's all.

没什么不得了的事！ méishénme bùdéliao de shì There's nothing seriously wrong.

有什么就凑合着用什么吧！ yǒu shé me jiù còuhé zhù yòng shénme ba Let's make do with what we have.

你懂什么！ Nǐ dǒng shénme! What do you know!

小屁孩，你懂什么！ Xiǎo pì hái, nǐ dǒng shénme! Little fart, what do you know! Little butt, what do you know!

你什么都不懂！ Nǐ shénme dōu bù dǒng! You do not understand anything! (You what all don't know (Lit))

多少 duōshǎo (代) 1 how many; how much: HSK 1 new

多少 duōshǎo   (副) 2 somewhat; more or less; to some extent: HSK 3 new

他讲的多少有点道理   tā jiǎng de duōshǎo yǒudiǎn dàolǐ   There's something in what he says

他多少有点不高兴   tā duōshǎo yǒudiǎn bù gāoxìng He's not entirely happy about it.

多少 duōshǎo   (代) 3 how many; how much: HSK 1 new

有多少人来参加晚会? yǒu duōshǎo rén lái cānjiā wǎnhuì?   How many people are corning to the party?

他干了多少了?   Tā gànle duōshǎole?   How much has he done?

多少 Duōshǎo   (代) 4 [used to indicate an uncertain quantity] :   HSK 3 new

我说过多少遍了,叫你别去那儿!   wǒ shuōguò duōshǎo biànle, jiào nǐ bié qù nà'er! Didn' t I tell you not to go there!

他懂多少! Tā dǒng duōshǎo! How much does he know!

几   jǐ   (代) how many (less than ten); few;   HSK 1 new

几　　jǐ　　　1（数）how many

今天星期几？　　jīntiān xīngqí jǐ?　　What day (of the week) is it today?

今天星期日。　　Jīntiān xīngqírì　　Today sunday

商店几点关门？　shāngdiàn jǐ diǎn guānmén?　　When does the shop close?

每天吃几次？　　Měitiān chī jǐ cì?　　How many times a day?

你要几号的鞋？　nǐ yào jǐ hào de xié?　　What size shoe would you like?

今天几号？--十三号。　jīntiān jǐ hào? --Shísān hào.　　What date is it today? --The 13th.

他几岁？　　Tā jǐ suì?　　he how old? (Lit.) How old is he?

你几点起床？　　Nǐ jǐ diǎn qǐchuáng?　　you what time get up?

现在几点？　　Xiànzài jǐ diǎn?　　now what time?

几点钟了？　　jǐ diǎn zhōngle?　　What's the time?

你能在这里住几天？　Nǐ néng zài zhèlǐ zhù jǐ tiān?　　How many days can you stay here?

现在几比几？　　xiànzài jǐ bǐ jǐ?　　What's the score?　HSK 3

几　　jǐ　　（代）2 a few; several; some:　　HSK 3

说几句话。shuō jǐ jù huà　　say a few words.

我在那里多住了几天。wǒ zài nàlǐ duō zhùle jǐ tiān　　I stayed there a few days longer.

几十　　　　　　　jǐshí　　　　　　　tens; dozens; scores.

十几岁的孩子。　shí jǐ suì de háizi　teenager.

二十几个人。　　èrshí jǐ gèrén　　twenty odd people

所剩无几。suǒ shèng wújǐ　There is not much left.

几分　jǐ fēn　(形) a bit; somewhat; rather:

她说的有几分道理。　tā shuō de yǒu jǐ fēn dàolǐ　There is a grain of truth in what she said.

几分怀疑　jǐ fēn huáiyí　be somewhat suspicious.

有几分醉意yǒu jǐ fēn zuìyì　be a bit tipsy

几时　jǐshí　(代) what time; when:　HSK 6

你们几时回来?　nǐmen jǐ shí huílái?What time will you come back?

怎么　Zěnme　1 (代) [interrogative pronoun]　HSK 1　new

怎　zěn　(代) why; how:

你怎才来呀?　nǐ zěn cái lái ya?　Why are you so late?

你怎么啦? nǐ zěnme la?　What's wrong with you?

请问, 去车站怎么走?　Qǐngwèn, qù chēzhàn zěnme zǒu?　Excuse me, but how can I get to the railway station?

你怎么没去开会? Nǐ zěnme méi qù kāihuì? Why didn't you attend the meeting?

这个词怎么拼? Zhège cí zěnme pīn? How do you spell the word?

怎么 Zěnme 2 [indicating the nature, condition and manner in general]:

你愿意怎么办就怎么办 nǐ yuànyì zěnme bàn jiù zěnme bàn Do as you please.

怎么 zěnme 3 [used in the negative to indicate inadequacy]: HSK 2 YAO

这个地方我不怎么熟悉 zhège dìfāng wǒ bù zě me shúxī I am not quite familiar with the place.

怎么样 zěnme yang (代) how [used as a predicative or complement]; What's up HSK 1 new

跟我们一起去,怎么样? gēn wǒmen yīqǐ qù, zěnme yàng? How about going there together wi th us?

怎么样 Zěnme yàng 2 [used in the negative] : HSK 3 YAO

这旅馆并不怎么样 zhè lǔguǎn bìng bù zě me yàng This hotel is not so good as we expected

他画得也并不怎么样 tā huà dé yě bìng bù zě me yàng He is not a particularly good painter

不怎么样 bùzěmmayàng (副) (平平常常) not up to much; very indifferent; so-so HSK 4 YAO

他网球打得不怎么样。 tā wǎngqiú dǎ dé bù zě me yàng. he plays tennis only so so.

这幅画画得不怎么样。　Zhè fú huà huà dé bù zě me yàng.　this isn't much of a painting

怎么着　　zěnme zhe　1 (代) [used to inquire about an action or state] ：　HSK 5 YAO

我们都去, 你打算怎么着？　　wǒmen dōu qù, nǐ dǎsuàn zěnme zhe? We are all going. What about you?

她今天不大做声，是生气了还是怎么着？Tā jīntiān bù dà zuò shēng, shì shēngqìle háishì zěnme zhe?　She was quiet today . Was she angry or what?

怎么着　　Zěnmezhe　2 in any case;whatever happens:　　HSK 6 YAO

怎么着也得把试验搞下去　　zěnmezhe yě dé bǎ shìyàn gǎo xiàqù　The experiment must be carried on whatever happens.

怎样　zěnyàng　　(代) 1 how [same as" 怎么"]：HSK 2 YAO

这件事你怎样向她解释？　　zhè jiàn shì nǐ zěnyàng xiàng tā jiěshì?　　How are you going to explain this to her?

怎样　Zěnyàng　　2 how [same as "怎么样"]　　HSK 2 YAO

你近来怎样？　　nǐ jìnlái zěnyàng?　How have you been keeping?

为什么　　wèishéme　(代) why; why (or how) is it that　　HSK 2　new

你喜欢上什么课？为什么？ Nǐ xǐhuān shàng shénme kè? Wèishéme? What class do you like? Why? (Lit.) What class do you like? Why?

你为什么不告诉她呢？ Nǐ wèishéme bù gàosù tā ne? Why do not you tell her? (Lit) Why do not you tell her?

他们今天为什么不去小张家？ Tāmen jīntiān wèishéme bù qù xiǎo zhāng jiā? today they why not go to zhang's house? (Lit.) Why do not they go to zhang's house today?

你这是为什么？ nǐ zhè shì wèishéme? Why are you doing this?

"你为什么哭丧着脸？""我男朋友不理我了。" Why do you have such a long face? "My boyfriend doesn't want to see me any more." HSK 4 new

你为什么老装傻？ Why are you always acting the fool?

你为什么老是对我怒气冲冲的？ Why do you get so angry with me all the time (= very often)?

我不明白他为什么生气。 I don't understand what he's angry about.

1.4 其他代词 Others

等(等)　　　děng　(代) and so on; etc.:　　　HSK 4　new

等　　děng　5　and so on; etc.:

等等　děng děng　　and so on; and so on and so forth; etc

等等　děng děng　　3 (动) wait; await:

梨、苹果、葡萄等　　　lí, píngguǒ, pútáo děng　　pears, apples, grapes and so on

等　　děng　6 [used to end an enumeration] :

北京、上海、广州等大城市　běijīng, shànghǎi, guǎngzhōu děng dà chéngshì

　　　　big cities such as Beijing, Shanghai, and Guangzhou

各　　gè　　(代) each; every:　HSK 4　new

各位先生女士　　gèwèi xiānshēng nǚshì　　Ladies and gentlemen .

各国　gèguó each country.

各个　gège　1 (代) each; every; one by one:

各个方面　gège fāngmiàn　　every aspect

各个　gège　2 (副) separately:

各个击破　gège jípò　　destroy one by one

各…各…　gè…gè…　　1 each . . . his own . . . :

各走各的路 gè zǒu gè de lù　　each goes his own way

各…各… gè…gè… 2 all kinds of:

各行各业 gè háng gè yè all walks of life

各式各样 gè shì gè yàng (形) of various kinds

各自 gèzì (代) each; respective: HSK 5 new

既要各自努力，也要彼此帮助 jì yào gèzì nǔlì, yě yào bǐcǐ bāngzhù This calls for both individual effort and mutual help.

各自为政 gèzìwéizhèng each acts wilfully regardless of overall interest

俩 liǎ (代) (口) two (of people) HSK 4 new

咱俩 zán liǎ we two; the two of us

俩 liǎ 2 some; several:

就这么俩人？ jiù zhème liǎ rén? Just these few people?

他们俩很合得来 。 tāmen liǎ hěn hédélái The two of them are getting along very well.

他俩的关系不好。 tā liǎ de guānxì bù hǎo. They are not on good terms with each other. or They don't get along.

他俩唱的是一个腔调。 tā liǎ chàng de shì yīgè qiāngdiào The two of them sing the same tune.

他们俩交情很深。 tāmen liǎ jiāoqing hěn shēn The two of them are just great friends.

他们俩很谈得来。   tāmen liǎ hěn tán dé lái   They get along well with each other

他们俩形影不离。   tāmen liǎ xíngyǐngbùlí.   They are always together

其次 qícì   (代) next; secondly; then: HSK 4 new

首先要重视内容还要注意文风   Pay attention first of all to the content, and then the style

质量是主要的，数量还在其次.   Quality is primary while quantity is of secondary importance.

想学好外语，首先要多听，其次要多说。   To learn a foreign language well, one should first listen to it more; and secondly speak it more.

我买东西，首先考虑质量，其次才考虑价格。   When I go shopping, my first concern is the quality, then the price.

我还不想走——首先，我没有准备好，其次，正在下雨。   I don't want to go yet - in the first place I'm not ready, and in the second place it's raining.

任何 rènhé   (代) any; whatever: HSK 4 new

没有任何希望。   méiyǒu rènhé xīwàng   There isn't any hope.

他没有任何理由不去。   tā méiyǒu rènhé lǐyóu bu qù   He has no reason whatsoever not to go.

我一整天都没跟任何人说句话。　　　　　I haven't spoken to anyone all day.

我没有告诉任何人。　　　　I haven't told anyone.

任何一门考试不通过，他都担负不起。　　　　He can ill afford to fail any of his exams.

对于我们的要求，我们不希望有任何含糊其词的地方。　　　　We wish to remove any ambiguity concerning our demands.

这个岛上没有任何动物生存。　　　　The island was devoid of all animal life (= there were no animals on the island).

我们不希望出现任何问题。　　　　We don't anticipate any trouble.

他吃任何含有小麦的食物，都会很不舒服。　　　　If he eats anything with wheat in it he's very sick.

不惜任何代价。　　　　at any cost; at all costs

任何事情都是有利有弊的，所以让人有时候很难取舍。　　　　Everything has both advantages and disadvantages, and therefore sometimes it's hard to make a choice.

所有　suǒyǒu　　　1 (代) all; what you have　　　HSK 4　new

所有　suǒyǒu　　　2 (名) possessions:

尽其所有　jìn qí suǒyǒu　　　give everything one has

所有　suǒyǒu　　　1 (代) all; what you have

把所有的劲儿都使出来。　　　bǎ suǒyǒu de jìn er dōu shǐ chūlái　　　exert all one's strength

所有制　　　suǒyǒuzhì　　（名）system of ownership; ownership

所有权　　　suǒyǒuquán（名）proprietary rights; ownership; title; proprietorship

所有的灯都灭了，我吓得六神无主。　　　I shit my pants when all the lights went out.

这个理论适应于所有学科。　　　This theory applies to every discipline.

关闭所有商店。　　　Close all the shops.

应该给所有候选人平等的机会才合理。　　　It's only right that all the candidates should be given a fair crack of the whip.

所有的学生都按能力进行编组。　　　Students are all put in different groups according to their ability.

所有知道她作品的人都认为她是个天才。　　　She was accounted a genius by all who knew her work.

一无所有　　　be destitute or penniless

咱们　zánmen　　（代）we [including both the speaker and the person or persons spoken to]　HSK 4 new

咱　zán　　（代）we, us, our　　V2020

咱班　zán bān　　（代）our class　　V2020

咱们 zánmen   (代) we, us V2020

咱们要努力把汉语学好   we should try our best to learn Chinese

另外 lìngwài   (代) in addition; moreover; besides; other; another HSK 4 new

我们属于另外一个组织   We belong to another organization.

某   mǒu   (代) certain; some: HSK 5 new

某人 mǒu rén   a certain person .

某日 mǒu rì   at a certain date

在某种程度上   zài mǒu zhǒng chéngdù shàng   to some (or a certain) extent 在某种意义上   zài mǒu zhǒng yìyì shàng   in a sense

某某   mǒu mǒu   (代) so-and-so:

某某大夫 mǒu mǒu dàfū   Dr. so-and-so; a certain doctor. V2020

某某学校 mǒu mǒu xuéxiào a certain school

某男   mǒu nán   John Doe

某女   mǒu nǚ   Jane Doe

某些   mǒuxie   certain; a few; some

在某些条件下   zài mǒu xiē tiáojiàn xià   on certain conditions

2 数词　shù cí　Numeral

2.1 表示时间　Biǎoshì shíjiān Express time

八点四十分　　　bā diǎn sìshí fēn　8:40

早上八点四十分　zǎoshang bā diǎn sìshí fēn　8:40 AM

晚上八点四十分	wǎnshàng bā diǎn sìshí fēn	8:40 PM
下午三点	xiàwǔ sān diǎn	3:00 PM in the afternoon
中午十二点	zhōngwǔ shí'èr diǎn	12 o'clock at noon
二零二零年六月十八日	Èr líng èr líng nián liù yuè shíbā rì	June 18, 2020
2020 年 6 月 18 日	Èr líng èr líng nián liù yuè shíbā rì	June 18, 2020

More time expression

点	diǎn	13[5] [used to indicate time] : o'clock
五点钟	wǔ diǎn zhōng	five o'clock
几点了？	jǐ diǎnle?	What time is it now?
到点了！	Dào diǎnle!	It's time!
一点钟	Yī diǎn zhōng	one o'Clock
两点钟	Liǎng diǎn zhōng	two o'clock

分 （钟[6]）	fēn (zhōng)	minute
分	fēn	7 (of time or degree) minute (= 1/60 of an hour or degree)
一分 （钟）	yī fēnzhōng	one minute

[5] 13 indicates the 13 meaning in our dictionary collection

[6] You can use 分 or 分钟

秒 （钟）	Miǎo (zhōng)	(量) second (= 1/ 60 of a minute)	
一秒 （钟）	Yī miǎo (zhōng)	one second	
五点十分	Wǔ diǎn shí fēn	5:10	HSK 3 new
五点过十分	Wǔ diǎn guò shí fēn	10 Pass Five	HSK 3 new
差十分五点	Chà shí fēn wǔ diǎn	10 Minutes to Five	HSK 5 new

火车三点钟到. huǒchē sān diǎn zhōng dào. The train arrives at three o'clock.

一点五 yīdiǎn wǔ one point five (1.5)

星期	xīng qí	Week	
星期	xīngqí	(名) week:	HSK 1 new
星期一	xīng qí yī	Monday	HSK 2 new
周一	zhōu yī	Monday	HSK 3 YAO
周日	zhōu rì	Sunday	HSK 3 YAO
周末	zhōumò	Weekend	HSK 3 new

2.2　表示年龄　　Biǎoshì niánlíng　　Express age

她今年 24 岁　　　Tā jīnnián 24 suì　She is 24 years old this year

年龄　　　　　　niánlíng　　　　　age　　HSK 4　new

您多大了？　　　nín duōdà suìshule?　　How old are you?

您多大岁数了？　nín duōdà suìshule?　　How old are you?

他几岁？　　　　Tā jǐ suì?　　　　　　How old is he?

2.3　表示钱数　　biǎoshì qián shù　　Express money

15 块　　　shíwǔ kuài　　　　15 dollar (or Yuan)

六元　　　　liù yuán　　　　　6 dollar (or Yuan)

多少钱？　　Duōshǎo qián?　　（代）how much?

这个多少钱？　　　　How much is this?

这几本书总共要多少钱？　How much do these books cost in total?

这条裤子你花了多少钱？　How much did you spend on these pants?

鱼多少钱一斤？　　　How much is a Jin of fish?

2.4 表示号码 biǎoshì hàomǎ Indicate Telephone number

我的电话是 587964123   My phone number is 587964123

2.5 表示顺序 biǎoshì shùnxù Express cardinal number

第一 dì yī (数) the first   HSK 2 new

2.6 表示重量 biǎoshì zhòngliàng Express weight

九公斤 jiǔ gōngjīn   Nine kilograms

2.7 表示长度 biǎoshì chángdù Express length

一千五百米 yīqiān wǔbǎi mǐ   One thousand five hundred meters

2.8 表示概数 biǎoshì gài shù Express an approximate figure

四五千人 sìwǔqiān rén   Four or five thousand people

八百多人 bābǎi duō rén   More than 800 people

2.9 Use of 二 and 两

两 liǎng   1 (数) two (used with measure word or quantity words): HSK 2 new

两间房子 liǎng jiān fángzi   two rooms.

两党制　　liǎngdǎngzhì　　　bipartisan system.

两百　　　liǎng bǎi　　two hundred

两　　　　liǎng　2 both (sides):

两相情愿　liǎngxiāngqíngyuàn　　both parties are willing

一厢情愿　　wishful thinking; base on [indulge in] one's own wishful thinking; one-sided wish; only one party is willing.; single consent; unilateral willingness; wishful thinking of one's own

两　　　liǎng　　　3 a few; some:

我过两天再来　wǒguò liǎng tiān zàilái　I'll come again in a couple of days

让我讲两句 ràng wǒ jiǎng liǎng jù　Let me say a few words.

两难　liǎngnán　　(形) be unable to decide between two unpleasant choices:

进退两难　jìntuìliǎngnán　　be in a dilemma; be (caught) between a rock and a hard place ; be in a cleft stick

两手　　　liǎngshǒu　(名) dual tactics:

作两手准备 zuò liǎngshǒu zhǔnbèi　prepare oneself for both eventualities

两性　　　liǎngxìng　　　(名) both sexes:

两性关系　　liǎngxìng guānxì　　sexual relations

2.10 Approximate numbers 概数

大概　　　　　　dàgài　　　　1 (形) general; rough; approximate:

一个大概印象　　yīgè dàgài yìnxiàng　　　　a general impression

大概数字　　　　dàgài shùzì　　　　　an approximate figure

大概　　　　　　dàgài　　　　2 (副) probably:

他大概病了　　　tā dàgài bìngle　　He is probably ill

大概　　　　　　dàgài　　　　3 (名) general idea:

我只记了个大概　wǒ zhǐ jìle gè dàgài　　　I have only some rough idea.

两三天　　liǎng sān tiān　　Two or three days

七八个　　qībā gè　　Seven or eight

四五天　　sìwǔ tiān　　Four or five days

七七八八　　qī qī bā bā　　almost done

十之八九　　shí zhī bā jiǔ　　Nine times out of ten; Almost always happens

八九不离十 bā jiǔ bùlí shí   pretty close; most likely; about right; most probably

三三两两   sānsān liǎng liǎng   in twos and threes

三天两头   sān tiān liǎngtóu   (口) almost every day

三心二意   sānxīn'èryì   1 be of two minds; shilly-shally:

别三心二意了   bié sānxīn'èryìle   Don't shilly-shally

三心二意   sānxīn'èryì   2 half-hearted

三言两语   sānyánliǎngyǔ   in a few words; in one or two words:

我们怎能把这事的原委用三言两语说清楚呢?   How could we explain the whole thing in just a few words?

三…四… sān… sì…   [indicating dis-order] :

颠三倒四   diānsāndǎosì   incoherent; disorganized.

丢三落四   diūsānlàsì   always be forgetting or mislaying things

七上八下   qī shàng bā xià   be agitated; be perturbed

七嘴八舌   qī zuǐ bā shé   with everybody trying to get a word in

一连两三天, 她不时专心致志地思考着这一问题, 但是毫无头绪, 以失败而告终。   She gave it her best thought from time to time, for two or three days—but it baffled her—defeated her.

此后的两三天好不容易才挨了过去。　　　　The next two or three days dragged by heavily .

乱七八糟　luànqībāzāo　　　　(形) at sixes and sevens; in a mess; in terrible disorder, at sixes and sevens (informal , old-fashioned) in us 乱七八糟，杂乱无章 in a confused, badly organized, or difficult situation

连包装一共有七八斤重。　　　　The weight is seven or eight pounds including package.

三令五申　sānlìngwǔshēn　　　repeated injunctions

三六九等　sānliùjiǔ děng　　　minute distinction of grades and ranks

三教九流　sānjiàojiǔliú　　　1 various religious sects and academic schools

三教九流　sānjiàojiǔliú　　　2 people of all sorts

三九天　sānjiǔ tiān　(名) the third nine-day period after the winter solstice - the coldest days of winter

三句话不离本行　sān jù huà bùlí běn háng　can hardly open one's mouth without talking shop; talk shop all the time

3 量词　liàng cí　quantifier; Measure words

Classifier (量词): A classifier is a word or affix that accompanies nouns and can be considered to "classify" a noun depending on the type of its referent. It is also sometimes called a measure word or counter word. (Wikipedia). There are around 120 Classifiers (量词) in Chinese language.

3.1 用在数词后　yòng zài shù cí hòu　Used after numerals

一个　　　　yīgè　　　　One (个 is the most common one, if you can not find proper one, use this one for safty).

三本书　　sān běn shū　　　　Three books

等一下	děng yīxià	Wait a moment
一双鞋	yīshuāng xié	a pair of shoes
两条鱼	liǎng tiáo yú	Two fish
第十层	dì shí céng	Tenth floor
三角五分	sānjiǎo wǔ fēn	three Jiao and five cents
两种	liǎng zhǒng	Two types

3.2 用在"这" "那" "几" "每"词后   Used after "this" "that" "several" "every"

这个	zhège	This one
那些	nàxiē	Those ones
几本	jǐ běn	Few (books)
每次	měi cì	Each (time)

3.3 其他   qítā other

| 他坐了一会儿。 | tā zuòle yīhuǐ'er. | He sat for a while. |
| 快一点儿。 | Kuài yīdiǎn er. | faster little bit; Hurry up |

3.4 自我描述量词 Self-descriptive quantifiers (日、周、年、天)

Self-descriptive quantifiers not need quantifier:

一日

一周

一年

一天

3.5 List of quantifier (量词 Measure words) by HSK levels

个   gè   (量) [the measure word most extensively used esp. before nouns which do not have special measure words of their own]:   HSK 1 new

一个人   yīgèrén   one person.

两个桃   liǎng gè táo   two peaches

三个星期   sān gè xīng qí   three weeks

四个问题   sì gè wèntí   four problems

个   gè   2 [used between a verb and its object] :

洗个澡   xǐ gè zǎo   have a bath.

理个发   lǐ gè fā   have a haircut

个   gè   3 [used before a numeral to indicate approximation] :

有个二十分钟就够了 　　yǒu gè èrshí fēnzhōng jiù gòule 　　About twenty minutes would be enough.

这手艺得干个三年才能学会 　　zhè shǒuyì dé gàn gè sān nián cáinéng xuéhuì One will need about three years to learn the skill.

个 　　　　　gè 　　4 [used between a verb and its complement]:

他说个不停 　　　tā shuō gè bù tíng 　　　He talked on and on.

明天我们要玩个痛快 　　míngtiān wǒmen yào wán gè tòngkuài 　　We'll have a wonderful time tomorrow.

一个大人 　yīgè dàrén 　　　An adult

一个小孩 　yīgè xiǎohái 　　　A child

一个女孩 　yīgè nǚhái 　　　A girl

一个男孩 　yīgè nánhái 　　　A boy

一个画家 　yīgè huàjiā 　　　A painter

一个司机 　yīgè sījī 　　　A driver

一个工人 　yīgè gōngrén 　　　A worker

一个农民 　yīgè nóngmín 　　　A farmer

一个士兵 　yīgè shìbīng 　　　A soldier

一个朋友 　yīgè péngyǒu 　　　A friend

岁	suì	(量) year (of age): HSK 1 new	
三岁女孩	sān suì nǔhái	a three-year-old girl	
她才五岁	tā cái wǔ suì	She is only five years old	
五十多岁	wǔshí duō suì	over fifty years old .	
十几岁的孩子	shí jǐ suì de háizi	teenager.	
五十来岁	wǔshí lái suì	over fifty (years old)	
四十岁上下	sìshí suì shàngxià	about forty years old	
他几岁？	tā jǐ suì?	How old is he?	

本	běn	(量) [for books, albums, etc.] HSK 1 new	
两本书	liǎng běn shū	two books	
一本笔记本	yī běn bǐjìběn	A notebook	
一本日记	yī běn rìjì	A diary	
一本账	yī běn zhàng	A account book.	
一本名册	yī běn míngcè	A roster （a list of people's names）	

些	xiē (量) some HSK 1 new	
这些	zhèxiē	these.

好些　　　　hǎoxiē　　　1 quite a few (or lot).

前些日子　　qián xiē rìzi recently.

写些信　　　xiě xiē xìn　write a few letters

有些　　　　yǒuxiē　　　1.(有的) some

有些人　　　yǒuxiē rén　some people;

有些学生在看书, 有些学生在听广播。　　yǒuxiē xuéshēng zài kànshū, yǒuxiē xuéshēng zài tīng guǎngbò.　　some students were reading, some were listening to the radio.

有些　　　　yǒuxiē　　　2.(有一些) somewhat; rather

有些不好意思　　yǒuxiē bù hǎoyìsi　be somewhat embarrassed;

有些失望　yǒuxiē shīwàng　be rather disappointed

有一些　　　yǒu yīxiē　　somewhat; rather

块　　kuài　　1 (量) [for a slice or chunk of sth.] 2 (名) piece; lump; cube; chunk; 2　　HSK 1　new

石块　shí kuài　　blocks of stone.

冰块　bīng kuài　　ice cubes

块　　kuài　　　　2 (量) [for a slice or chunk of sth.] :

三块巧克力 sān kuài qiǎokèlì   three chocolate bars

巧克力   qiǎokèlì   chocolate

一块面包   yīkuài miànbāo   a piece of bread

两块肥皂   liǎng kuài féizào   two cakes of soap

块   kuài   3 (口) yuan , the basic unit of money in China:

三块钱   sān kuài qián   three yuan

次   cì   (量) time; occurrence   HSK 2 new

三次 sāncì three times

第二次   dì èr cì   the second time

首次   shǒucì   first time

上次   shàng cì   last time

下次   xià cì   next time

一次   yīcì   for one time; once:

我做过一次 wǒ zuòguò yīcì   I've done it once

再次 zàicì   (副) once more ; a second time; once again:

这次 zhè cì   (代) this time; present ; current:

这次会议 zhè cì huìyì   the present session.

这次会议英国大选   zhè cì huìyì yīngguó dàxuǎn   the current British general elections

公斤   gōngjīn   (量) kilogram (kg) HSK 2 new

净重 100 公斤   jìngzhòng 100 gōngjīn   Net weight is one hundred kg

你的行李超重五公斤。 Nǐ de xínglǐ chāo chóng wǔ gōngjīn. Your luggage Your luggage is overweighted five kilograms .

免费行李限额是二十公斤。   Miǎnfèi xínglǐ xiàn'é shì èrshí gōngjīn.   Free luggagee allowance is twenty kilos.

元   yuán   (量) dollar   HSK 2 new

元   yuán   yuan , the basic unit of money in China

欧元 ōuyuán   (名) the euro

美元 měiyuán   US dollar

日元 rì yuán   yen; Japanese yen

角　　Jiǎo　classfier fractional unit of currency in China, equal to one tenth of one yuan

三元八角二分　　sān yuán bājiǎo èrfēn　　three yuan and eighty-two fen

五角钱　　wǔjiǎo qián five jao

我借给他 50 元钱。　　wǒ jiè gěi tā 50 yuán qián.　　I lent him fifty yuan

1 元等于 100 分。 1 yuán děngyú 100 fēn.　One yuan equals a hundred fen

一元是十角，一角是十分。　Yīyuán shì shí jiǎo, yījiǎo shì shífēn.　One yuan is ten Jiao, one Jiao is ten sens.

那个手机不到一千元。 Nàgè shǒujī bù dào yīqiān yuán.　　The phone is less than one thousand dollars. (Lit.)

三十块钱。 Sānshí kuài qián.　Thirty dollars.

三十元。　Sānshí yuán.Thirty yuan.

件　　jiàn　（量）[indicating those things which can be counted]:　　HSK 2 new

一件衣服　yī jiàn yīfú　　A piece of clothing

一件上衣　yī jiàn shàngyī　　A top (clothing)

一件事	yī jiàn shì	one thing
一个事件	yīgè shìjiàn	An event
一件大事	yī jiàn dàshì	A big event
两件家具	liǎng jiàn jiājù	Two pieces of furniture
一件衬衫	yī jiàn chènshān	a shirt.
两件事情	liǎng jiàn shìqíng	two things.
三件行李	sān jiàn xínglǐ	three pieces of luggage

件	jiàn	2 (名) letter; correspondence; paper; document:
信件	xìnjiàn	letters; mail
来件	lái jiàn	a communication, document, etc. received .
密件	mìjiàn	confidential (or classified) documents; secret papers

张　　　　zhāng　　　　1 (量) for flat things like paper, table, bed etc. HSK 2 new

一张桌子	yī zhāng zhuōzi	a table.
两张床	liǎng zhāng chuáng	two beds
一张纸	yī zhāng zhǐ	a piece of paper

张　　　　　　　zhāng　　　　　2 classifier. used for mouth, table or paper etc

两张嘴　　　　　　liǎng zhāngzuǐ　　　two mouths

三张照片儿　　　　sān zhāng zhào piān er　　three photos or three pictures

咱们照一张合影吧　　zánmen zhào yī zhāng héyǐng ba　　　Let's take a group photo

纸张　　　　zhǐzhāng　　　　　paper

一张餐纸　　yī zhāng cān zhǐ　　A piece of paper

一张桌子　　yī zhāng zhuōzi　　a table

一张弓　　　yī zhānggōng　　　A bow

一张纸　　　yī zhāng zhǐ　　　　A paper

一张地图　　yī zhāng dìtú　　　A map

两张画　　　liǎng zhāng huà　　Two paintings

三张木板　　sān zhāng mùbǎn　　Three planks

十张皮子　　shí zhāng pízi　　Ten skins

一张脸　　　yī zhāng liǎn　　　A face

一张嘴　　　yī zhāngzuǐ　A mouth

包　　bāo　　(量) [for packages, bundles, etc.];　bag:　HSK 3　new

一包香烟　yī bāoxiāngyān　a packet (or pack) of cigarettes.

一包棉纱　yī bāo miánshā　a bale of cotton yarn

包　　bāo　8 bag:

书包　shūbāo　　satchel; school bag

辆　　　　liàng　　　　(量) (for vehicles): HSK 3 new

一辆车　　yī liàng chē　　　a car

一辆汽车　yī liàng qìchē　　A car

一辆自行车　yī liàng zìxíngchē　　a bicycle

一辆卡车　yī liàng kǎchē　　a lorry

两辆轿车　liǎng liàng jiàochē　　two cars

车辆　　chēliàng　　　(名) vehicle; car

双　　shuāng　　(量) pair:　HSK 3 new

一双鞋　yīshuāng xié　　a pair of shoes

两双筷子　liǎng shuāng kuàizi　　two pairs of chopsticks

双　　shuāng　　1 (形) twin; both; dual:

双手　　　　shuāng shǒu　　　　both hands.

成双成对　　chéng shuāng chéng duì　in pairs

双　　　　　shuāng　　　　　　　2 even:

双数　　　　shuāng shù　　　　　even numbers

双　　　　　shuāng　　　　　　　3 double; twofold;

双人床　　　shuāngrén chuáng　　double bed.

双人房间　　shuāngrén fángjiān　　double room

种　　zhǒng　　　　(量) kind; type; sort:　　HSK 3 new

这种行为　　zhè zhǒng xíngwéi　　this kind of behaviour

好几种颜色　hǎo jǐ zhǒng yánsè　　different colours

各种情况　　gè zhǒng qíngkuàng　　various conditions

各种 gèzhǒng　　all kinds of; a combination of; a variety of; various kinds

各种各样 gèzhǒnggèyàng　　all sorts of, all kinds of; a great variety of; a variety of; all manner of; assorted; diverse; diversified; in various qualities; miscellaneous; multifarious; of all sorts; of every sort and kind; of sorts; variant;

种　　zhǒng　　　　1 (名) seed

种子 zhǒngzǐ　　(名) seed:

种种	zhǒngzhǒng	(形) all sorts of; a variety of.
由于种种原因	yóuyú zhǒngzhǒng yuányīn	for various reasons
想尽种种办法	xiǎng jǐn zhǒngzhǒng bànfǎ	try every means possible

条 tiáo (量) MW used for long and thin things or itemized nouns HSK 3
new

两条鱼	liǎng tiáo yú	two fish
三条船	sāntiáo chuán	three ships
两条路	liǎng tiáo lù	two roads
一条街	yītiáo jiē	a street
一条河	yītiáo hé	a river
一条狗	yītiáo gǒu	A dog
一条蛇	yītiáo shé	A snake
一条鱼	yītiáo yú	A fish
一条虫	yītiáo chóng	A worm
一条胳臂	yītiáo gēbei	An arm
一条腿	yītiáo tuǐ	One leg

一条绳子	yītiáo shéngzi	A rope
一条裤子	yītiáo kùzi	a pair of pants
一条路	yītiáo lù	one way
一条船	yītiáo chuán	A boat
一条江	yītiáo jiāng	A river
一条河	yītiáo hé	a river
一条线	yītiáo xiàn	a line
一条大河	yītiáo dàhé	A big river
一条大街	yītiáo dàjiē	A street
一条板凳	yītiáo bǎndèng	A bench
一条好汉	yītiáo hǎohàn	A hero
一条人命	yītiáo rénmìng	A life
一条香烟	yītiáo xiāngyān	a carton of cigarettes
两条新闻	liǎng tiáo xīnwén	two pieces of news
三条建议	sāntiáo jiànyì	three suggestions

碗   wǎn   (量) bowl; a bowl of   HSK 3 new

碗　　wǎn　　　　　1 n. bowl

碗　　wǎn　　　　　2 (量) a bowl of

一碗牛肉汁　　yī wǎn niúròu zhī　　　　a bowl of beef broth

一碗米饭　　yī wǎn lāmiàn　　　　a bowl of rice

一碗拉面　　yī wǎn lāmiàn　　　　a bowl of ramen

位　　wèi　　　　　(量) [polite form for a person]　HSK 3　new

四位客人　　sì wèi kèrén four guests

一位老师　　yī wèi lǎoshīa teacher

那位是谁?　　nà wèi shì shuí?　　Who is the one over there?

哪位　nǎ wèi　　who? (Which one?_

他是一位名作家。　　tā shì yī wèi míng zuòjiā.　　He is a renowned writer

大家都喜欢这位女教师。　　dàjiā dōu xǐhuān zhè wèi nǚ jiàoshī.　All of us like this female teacher

他是一位种菜大王。　　tā shì yī wèi zhòng cài dàwáng.　　He is the largest vegetable growers

倍　　bèi　　　　　(量) times: -fold:　HSK 4　new

四倍　sì bèi　　　　four times; fourfold.

增长了五倍　　zēngzhǎngle wǔ bèi　　increase by 500 % ; register a 500 % increase; be six times as much.

产量成倍增长　　chǎnliàng chéng bèi zēngzhǎng Output has doubled and redoubled.

倍　　bèi　　　　2 double; twice as much:

事半功倍　　shìbàngōngbèi　　get twice the result with half the effort

倍数　bèishù　　（名）multiple (a number that can be divided by a smaller number an exact number of times)

遍　　biàn　　　　（量）[indicating the process of an action from beginning to end] time, times　HSK 4　new

这本书我从头到尾看过两遍　zhè běn shū wǒ cóngtóu dào wěi kànguò liǎng biàn I've read the book twice from cover to cover,

请再说一遍　　qǐng zàishuō yībiàn　　　　Please say it again.

他又重复了一遍。　　tā yòu chóngfùle yībiàn.　He repeated it again

场　　chǎng　　　　（量）[said of something which has happened]　HSK 4　new

一场大雨　yī chǎng dàyǔ　　　　a heavy fall of rain

场　　　chǎng　　　4（量）[for sports and recreation]：

一场电影　　　yī chǎng diànyǐng　　　a film show

一场球赛　　　yī chǎng qiúsài　　　a ball game

一场风波　　　yī chǎng fēngbō　　　A storm (of problem); a disturbance; troubled waters

一场战争　　　yī chǎng zhànzhēng　　　A war

一场大火　　　yī chǎng dàhuǒ　　　A fire

顿　　　　　dùn　　　（量）（used for number of times of scold, meal, persuade ）
HSK 4　new

三顿饭　　　sān dùn fàn　　　three meals.

挨了一顿骂　āile yī dùn mà　　　get a scolding

饱餐一顿　　bǎocān yī dùn　　　have a big meal; eat and drink one's fill

一顿美餐　　yī dùn měicān　　　a delicious meal

一顿臭骂　　yī dùn chòumà　　　A scolding

臭骂　chòumà　　　（动）curse angrily：

挨了一顿臭骂　āile yī dùn chòumà get a dressing down

朵　　　　　duǒ　　　（量）(for flower, cloud)　　　HSK 4　new

一朵花　　yī duǒ huā　a flower.

一朵云　　yī duǒ yún　a cloud

一朵浪花　yī duǒ lànghuā　　A spray (a mass of very small drops of liquid carried in the air)

份　　fèn　　(量) (for gift, etc)　HSK 4　new

一份礼品　yī fèn lǐpǐn　　　a gift.

一份报纸　yī fèn bàozhǐ　　　a copy of a newspaper.

一份中国日报　yī fèn zhōngguó rìbào　　a copy of China Daily

一份早餐　yī fèn zǎocān　　　A breakfast

一份午餐　yī fèn wǔcān　　　A lunch

一份晚餐　yī fèn wǎncān　　　A dinner

一份中餐　yī fèn zhōngcān　　　A Chinese meal

一份西餐　yī fèn xīcān　　　A western meal

一份点心　yī fèn diǎnxīn　　　A snack

一份饭　　yī fèn fàn　　　A meal

一份礼　　yī fèn lǐ　　　A gift

一份杂志　　yī fèn zázhì　　　　A magazine

一份情意　　yī fèn qíngyì　　　　(a) love; affection; goodwill

棵　　kē　　（量）(used for trees, plants.)　　HSK 4 new

一棵树　　　yī kē shù　　　　A tree

一棵草　　　yī kē cǎo　　　　A grass

一棵松　　　yī kē sōng　　　　A pine

一棵葱　　　yī kē cōng　　　　A green onion

一棵大白菜　　yī kē dà báicài　　a (head of) Chinese cabbage

你能爬上这棵树吗？　　　　Can you climb up this tree?

这棵树结了很多果实。　　　This tree is bearing a lot of fruit

篇　　piān　　（量）a piece of writing; (for paper, article, etc.)　　HSK 4 new

一篇文章　　yī piān wénzhāng　a piece of writing; an essay

一篇报告　　yī piān bàogào　　A report

一篇论文　　yī piān lùnwén　　a dissertation

两篇报告　　liǎng piān bàogào　Two reports

一篇日记　　yī piān rìjì　　　　A diary

诗篇　　　　shīpiān　　　　　　2 (名) inspiring story

长篇小说　　chángpiān xiǎoshuō　　　novel.

中篇小说　　zhōng piān xiǎoshuō　　　novelette.

短篇小说　　duǎnpiān xiǎoshuō short story　HSK 4　new

废话连篇　　fèihuà liánpiān　　　　pages and pages of nonsense

这篇文章写得比较好。　　　　his article is comparatively well-written.

匹　　pǐ　　(量) [for horses, etc.]:　HSK 5　new

三匹马　　sān pǐ mǎ　　three horses

两匹骡子　　liǎng pǐ luózi　　Two mules

马匹　mǎ pǐ horse

匹　　pǐ　　3 [for cloth] :

一匹布　　yī pǐ bù　　a bolt of cloth

布匹　bùpǐ　(名) cloth; piece goods

片　　piàn　（量）[for things in slices]; (名) a flat; thin piece;　HSK 5　new

一片面包　yīpiànmiànbāo　　a slice of bread

两片药　　liǎng piàn yào　　two tahlets

药片　　　yàopiàn　　　　　(名) (medicinal) tablet, pill

一片嘴唇　yīpiàn zuǐchún　　A lip

一片叶子　yīpiàn yèzi　　　A leaf

一片肉　　yīpiàn ròu　　　　A piece of meat

一片面包　yīpiàn miànbāo　　A slice of bread

一片西瓜　yīpiàn xīguā　　　A slice of watermelon

片　　piàn　　　　（量) 4 [said of an expanse of land or water] :

一片汪洋　yīpiàn wāngyáng　a vast expanse of water

片　　piàn　　　　（量) [for scenery, weather, language, mood. etc.]:

一片欢腾　yīpiàn huānténg　　a scene of jubilation

一片漆黑　yīpiàn qīhēi　　　a pall of darkness.

一片繁荣景象　　yīpiàn fánróng jǐngxiàng　a glowing picture of prosperity

一片诚心　yīpiàn chéngxīn　　in all sincerity

一片好心　yīpiàn hǎoxīn　　　with the best of intentions
7荒凉　huāngliáng　　(形) bleak and desolate; wild:　　HSK 6　new

一片荒凉[7]   yīpiàn huāngliáng a scene of desolation

片   piàn   1 (名) a flat; thin piece;   HSK 5 new

皂片 zào piàn   soap flakes

雪片 xuěpiàn   snowflakes.

肉片 ròupiàn   sliced meat

眼镜片   yǎnjìng piàn   lens

唱片   chàngpiān   (名) record; disc:

卡片 kǎpiàn   (名) card:

薯条 Shǔ tiáo   (名) French fries

薯片 Shǔ piàn   (名) Potato chips

麦片 màipiàn   (名) oatmeal:

明信片   míngxìnpiàn (名) postcard

木片 mùpiàn   (名) wood chip

片   piàn   2 incomplete; fragmentary:

片言 piànyán   a few words

幅　　fú　　（量）[for cloth, painting, etc.] a piece　　HSK 5　new

幅　　fú　　1（名）width of cloth; size of a painting, photographs, etc.

一幅布　　yī fú bù　　a (piece of) cloth (with standard unit width)

幅　　fú　　2（量）[for cloth, painting, etc.] a piece

一幅画　　yī fú huà　　a picture; a painting

一幅照片　　yī fú zhàopiàn　　a photo

一幅地图　　yī fú dìtú　　a map

一幅照片　　yī fú zhàopiàn　　a photo

幅　　fú　　3（量）range: scope: extent

大幅攀升　　dàfú pānshēng　　a sharp increase.

篇幅　piānfú　　1（名）length (of a piece of writing)

篇幅　piānfú　　2 space (on a printed page) :

条幅　tiáofú　　banner

这幅油画意境深远。　　zhè fú yóuhuà yìjìng shēnyuǎn　This painting gives expression to a high level of artistic conception

幅度　　fúdù　　（名）range: scope: extent:

大幅增长　　dàfú zēngzhǎng　　increase by a big margin

粒　　lì　　(量) [for grain-like things] (名) grain; granule; pellet:　　HSK 5
new

砂粒　shālì　grains of sand

粒　　　　lì　　2 (量) [for grain-like things]

一粒米　　yī lì mǐ　　a grain of rice

三粒子弹　sān lìzǐdàn　　three bullets

一粒葡萄　yī lì pútáo　　A grape

一粒苹果　yī lì píngguǒ　　An apple

一粒糖果　yī lì tángguǒ　　A candy

每次服五粒　　měi cì fú wǔ lì　　5 pills each

一粒珠子　　yī lì zhūzi　　A bead

一粒沙　　yī lì shā　　a grain of sand

一粒药丸　　yī lì yàowán　　A pill

一粒盐　　yī lì yán　　a grain of salt

颗粒　　kēlì　1 (名) anything small and roundish (as a bean, pearl, etc.);
pellet

颗粒　　kēlì　2 grain:

颗粒归仓　　kēlì guī cāng　　　　every grain to the granary

一粒老鼠屎，坏了一锅粥。　　　　　　a speck of mouse dung will spoil a whole
pot of porridge.

届　　jiè　　（量）[used before a regular meeting or each year's graduates]: session;
year's HSK 5 new

届　　jiè　　2（量）[used before a regular meeting or each year's graduates]:

本届联大　　běn jiè lián dà　　　the present session of the U. N. General Assembly.

届　　jiè　　1（动）fall due:　　HSK 5 new

届期　jiè qí　when the day comes; on the appointed date

本届　　　běn jiè　　　　current; this year's:

本届毕业生　　　běn jiè bìyè shēng　　　this year's graduates

届满　　　jièmǎn　　　（动）at the expiration of one' s term of office:

任期届满　　rènqí jièmǎn The term of office has expired.

历届 lìjiè　（名）all previous (sessions, governments, etc.):

历届大会　　lìjiè dàhuì　　all previous conferences

连任两届总统　　　liánrèn liǎng jiè zǒngtǒng　　　be elected president for two consecutive terms

每届总统任期四年　　　měi jiè zǒngtǒng rènqí sì nián　　The president is elected for a term of four years.

团　　　　　　tuán　　（量）a ball of; a lump of　HSK 5　new

一团毛线　　yī tuán máoxiàn　　a ball of wool

一团面　　　yī tuán miàn　　　a lump of dough

面团　　　　miàntuán　　　　（名）dough

蛇盘成一团 shé pán chéngyī tuán　　The snake coiled up.

漆黑一团　qīhēi yī tuán pitchdark; be entirely ignorant of

挤做一团　jǐ zuò yī tuán　　　pressed close together; packed like sardines.

团　　tuán　　　　1（形）round; circular:

团扇　tuán shàn　　round fan

团　　tuán　　　　2（动）unite; conglomerate:

团结　tuánjié　　　unite with

团　　tuán　　　　3 (名) group; society; organization

抱团儿　　bàotuán er　　gang up; hang together

财团　　cáituán　　(名) financial group:

国际财团　guójì cáituán　　　consortium

集团　　jítuán (名) group; clique; circle; bloc: HSK 6 new

统治集团　tǒngzhì jítuán　　　the ruling clique; the ruling circle

旅行团　　lǔxíng tuán　(名) touring group.

马戏团　　mǎxì tuán　　circus troupe

批　　pī　　(量) batch; lot; group:　　HSK 5 new

新到的一批货物　xīn dào de yī pī huòwù　　a new lot of goods

批量生产　pīliàng shēngchǎn　　　batch production.

分两批走　fēn liǎng pī zǒu　　go (or leave) in two groups

成批　　chéng pī　　in batches; one group after another

大批　　dàpī　　(形) large quantities or number:

大批工厂　dàpī gōngchǎng　　a large number of factories.

大批金钱　dàpī jīnqián　a large sum (or amount) of money

批发　　　　pīfā　1 (动) wholesale (sell in batch or in large amounts at low prices to shops and businesses, rather than the selling of goods in shops to customers)

批发市场　Pīfā shìchǎng　　Wholesale market

小商品批发市场　xiǎoshāngpǐn pīfā shìchǎng　　Small commodity wholesale market

米　　　　　mǐ　3 (量) metre HSK 3　new

分米　　　　fēn mǐ　　　(名) decimetre (dm) 分米（十分之一米）

厘米　　　　límǐ　　　(量) centimeter　　HSK 5　new

公分　　　　gōngfēn　　(名) 1 centimetre (cm)

毫米　　　　háomǐ millimetre.　HSK 6　new

微米　　　　a micrometre (one millionth of the stated unit)　　HSK 7　new

纳米　　　　nanometre; nano (one billionth of metre)　　HSK 7　new

一块宽 22 厘米长 35 厘米的玻璃　　　　a piece of glass 22 cm by 35 cm

衣柜 2 米高，1 米宽，60 厘米深。　　The wardrobe is 2 m high, 1 m wide and 60 cm deep.

16 毫米的口径　　　　　　a bore of 16 millimetres

口径为 12 毫米的猎枪　　　a twelve-bore shotgun

她打破了 5000 米的纪录。　　She broke the record for the 5,000 metres.

这条河最开阔处有 500 多米宽。　　This river is over 500 metres broad at its widest point.

他 100 米跑了 10 秒。　　He clocked ten seconds in the 100 metres (= he ran it in ten seconds).

她在百米赛跑中得了第二。　　She came second (us came in second) in the 100 metres.

成年长颈鹿有 5.5 米高。　　A full-grown giraffe is 5.5 m tall.

这棵橡树干围长两米。　　The oak was two metres in girth.

它有两米半高，一米宽。　　It's two and a half metres high and one metre wide.

他身高 1.75 米。　　He is 1 m 75 tall.

她获得了奥运会 100 米短跑冠军。　　She won the 100 metres (= a race run over this distance) at the Olympics.

15 米长的游艇　　a 15-metre yacht

微米　　a micrometre

（直径）6 毫米的钻头　　a 6 mm (diameter) drill

血压读数为 127 / 78 毫米汞柱   A blood pressure reading of 127/78 mmHg

纳米技术   nanotechnology

纳米   nanometre; nano[8] (one billionth of metre)

颗   kē   (量) Classifier; Measure Word (MW) for a small and roundish (as a bean, pearl, etc.)   HSK 5 new

一颗珠子   yī kē zhūzi   a pearl.

一颗黄豆   yī kē huángdòu   a soya bean

一颗脑袋   yī kē nǎodai   A head

一颗牙齿   yī kē yáchǐ   A tooth

一颗心   yī kē xīn   a heart

一颗种子   yī kē zhǒngzǐ   A seed

一颗星星   yī kē xīngxīng   A star

一颗黄豆   yī kē huángdòu   A soybean

一颗子弹   yī kē zǐdàn   A bullet

一颗牙齿   yī kē yáchǐ   A tooth

颗粒 kēlì   1 (名) anything small and roundish (as a bean, pearl, etc.); pellet

---

[8] nano-   prefix SCIENCE specialized UK /næn.əʊ-/ US /næn.oʊ-/ 十亿分之一的 one billionth of the stated unit

颗粒　kēlì　2 grain:

食物颗粒　food pellets

颗粒归仓　kēlì guī cāng　every grain to the granary

我悬着一颗心，备受煎熬。　I was in an agony of suspense.

一颗子弹嵌进了男孩的腿里。　A bullet had lodged in the boy's leg.

他面部被击中以后，掉了两颗牙齿。　Two of his teeth came out after he got hit in the face.

那颗牙终于拔掉了。　The tooth was eventually extracted.

她有一颗金子般的心。　She has a heart of gold.

木星至少有 16 颗卫星。　Jupiter has at least 16 moons.

那颗石子咚的一声掉进了水里。　The stone fell into the water with a plop.

两颗子弹近距离射进了轿车。　Two bullets were fired into the car at point-blank range.

牙医把两颗牙都拔了出来。　The dentist pulled both teeth out.

一颗大红宝石戒指　a ring with a large ruby

他把一颗葡萄放进嘴里，整个儿吞了下去。　He put a grape into his mouth and swallowed it whole.

肉眼应该能看见那颗彗星。　The comet should be visible to the naked eye.

昨天一颗重 15 公吨的卫星被成功送入了轨道。　　Yesterday a satellite weighing 15 tons was successfully placed in orbit.

4 副词　fùcí　　Adverb

4.1 否定副词：　fǒudìng fùcí:　Negative adverb:

不　　bù　　(副) [used to form a negative] no, not　HSK 1　new

我不是学生。　　wǒ bùshì xuéshēng.　　I'm not a student.

没　méi　(副) not have; be without　HSK 1　new

他没去医院。　　tā méi qù yīyuàn.　He did not go to the hospital.

别　bié　(副) don't (used before verb)

你别去游泳了。　nǐ bié qù yóuyǒngle.　　Don't go swimming.

一定 yīdìng　　(副) certainly; surely; necessarily:　　HSK 3　new

我明天一定来。　wǒ míngtiān yīdìng lái.　I must come tomorrow.

必须　　　　bìxū　(动) must; have to:　　　HSK 3 new

我们必须想个好办法。　　　We must think of a good way.

4.2　程度副词：　　Chéngdù fùcí: Degree adverb:

很　　hěn　(副) very; quite; awfully:　　　HSK 1 new

他很高兴。tā hěn gāoxìng.　　He is very happy.

太　　tài　(副) excessively; too; over:　　HSK 1 new

太好了　　　tài hǎole　　Great

非常　　　　fēicháng　　(副) very; extremely; highly　　HSK 2 new

那里的天气非常热。　　　The weather there is very hot.

最　　zuì　(副) [indicating the superlative degree]:　　HSK 2 new

我最喜欢喝咖啡。　　　I like coffee most. V2020

更　　gèng　　(副) even; more; still more; further:　　HSK 3 new

明天会更好。　　　Tomorrow will be better.

越 + Verb + 越 + (Adjective, Adverb, or short phrase as complement for the verb, state of action) (YAO Style formula)

越　　yuè　　　　(副) all the more; even more:　HSK 3　new

越…越…　　　　yuè…yuè… (副) the more... the more. …

雨越下越大。　　yǔ yuè xiàyuè dà.　The rain is getting heavier.

越多越好　　　yuè duō yuè hǎo　　　　the more the better

愈来愈… = 越来越…　yù lái yù …　　　more and more ...

越来越… + Adjective (YAO Style formula)

越来越… …　　　Yuè lái yuè… …　　(副) More and more...

天越来越黑了。　tiān yuè lái yuè hēile.　　It is getting darker.

她越来越漂亮。　Tā yuè lái yuè piàoliang. She was more beautiful.

他长得越来越高。　　Tā zhǎng dé yuè lái yuè gāo.　He grows more and more taller.

这孩子吃得越来越多　Zhè háizi chī dé yuè lái yuè duō This child eat more and more

往后的天气越来越冷了。　Wǎng hòu de tiānqì yuè lái yuè lěngle. It 's getting colder and colder from now on .

问题越来越大了。　Wèntí yuè lái yuè dàle. The problem is beginning to assume massive proportions.

随着冬天来临，白天越来越短了。　Suízhe dōngtiān láilín, báitiān yuè lái yuè duǎnle. The days get shorter as winter approaches.

4.2.1　More Adverbs in GCSE Syllabus

A　Sentences with an adverbial phrase before the verb

Point of time

他昨天去了上海。　tā zuótiān qùle shànghǎi. He went to Shanghai yesterday.

他明天要去上海。　tā míngtiān yào qù shànghǎi. He is going to Shanghai tomorrow.

Place

她在西安学习英语。　tā zài xī'ān xuéxí yīngyǔ. She is studying English in Xi'an.

Manner

他们坐船去。　tāmen zuò chuán qù. They go by boat.

他们坐飞机去。　　tāmen zuò fēijī qù.　　　　They go by plane.

Frequency

我们常常去便利店。　　wǒmen chángcháng qù biànlì diàn.　　We often go to convenience stores.

我们不常去超市。　　Wǒmen bù cháng qù chāoshì.　　We don't often go to the supermarket.

Other adverbs

她也来。　　tā yě lái.　　　　She also come.

我也去。　　wǒ yě qù.　　　　I am coming too.

你也知道。　nǐ yě zhīdào.　　You know too.

我也明白。　wǒ yě míngbái.　　I also understood.

Movement

他从南京到上海去。　　tā cóng nánjīng dào shànghǎi qù.　　　He went to Shanghai from Nanjing.

他从南京坐船到上海去。　　tā cóng nánjīng zuò chuán dào shànghǎi qù.　He took a boat from Nanjing to Shanghai.

Prepositional phrases

他给他弟弟写信。　　tā gěi tā dìdì xiě xìn.　　He wrote to his brother.

他给他爸爸打电话。　　tā gěi tā bàba dǎ diànhuà.　He called his dad.

他经常给他爸爸打电话。　　　　tā jīngcháng gěi tā bàba dǎ diànhuà.　He often calls his father.

Conjunctive use of adverbs

他又饿又累。　　　tā yòu è yòu lèi.　He was hungry and tired.

她来, 她弟弟也来。　　　tā lái, tā dìdì yě lái. She came, so did her brother.

B Sentences with an adverbial phrase after the verb
Complement of time after the verb

他住三天。　　　tā zhù sān tiān.　He lived (will live) for three days.

他要住三天。　　　tā yào zhù sān tiān. He will live for three days

Complement of time with the verbal aspect marker 了

他住了三天。　　　tā zhùle sān tiān.　He lived for three days.

他已经住了三天。　　　tā yǐjīng zhùle sān tiān.　He has lived for three days already.

Complement of time with the verbal aspect
marker 了 and the sentence particle 了

他住了三天了。　　　　tā zhùle sān tiānle.

Repetition of the verb

她学法语学了两年。　　　tā xué fǎyǔ xuéle liǎng nián.　　　She studied French for two years.

她打篮球打了两个小时。　　　tā dǎ lánqiú dǎle liǎng gè xiǎoshí.　　　She played basketball for two hours.

她打游泳游了一个小时。　　　tā dǎ yóuyǒng yóule yīgè xiǎoshí　　　She played swimming for an hour.

Verb + 得 + (Adjective, complement for the verb, state of action) (YAO Style formula)

她打篮球打了两个小时。　　　tā dǎ lánqiú dǎle liǎng gè xiǎoshí.　　　She played basketball for two hours.

她打游泳游了一个小时。　　　tā dǎ yóuyǒng yóule yīgè xiǎoshí　　　She played swimming for an hour.

Verb followed by postverb

她住在广州。　　　tā zhù zài guǎngzhōu.　　　She lives in Guangzhou.

Verb followed by 得 and a complement of degree

小孩子走得很慢。　　　xiǎo háizi zǒu dé hěn màn.　　　The children walk very slowly.

Verb + 得 + (Adjective, complement for the verb, state of action) (YAO Style formula)

得　　de　　1 (助)[used between a verb or an adjective and its complement to indicate result, possibility or degree]

走得快　　zǒu de kuài　　walk fast.

唱得好　　chàng de hǎo　　sing well

办得到　　bàn dedào　　it can be done

拿得动　　ná de dòng　　can carry i t.

雪下得大　xuě xià de dà　　It snowed heavily.

病得厉害　bìng de lìhài　　be very ill.

好得很　　hǎo de hěn　　very good.

冷得打哆嗦 lěng de dǎ duōsuō　shiver with cold

得　　dé　　2 (助) [used after certain verbs to indicate possibility] :

这种蘑菇吃得　　zhè zhǒng mógū chī dé　　This kind of mushroom is edible

衬衣太短，穿不得了　　chènyī tài duǎn, chuān bùdéle　　The shirt is too short for me now.

这话可说不得.　　zhè huà kě shuōbudé.　　We (You) mustn't say things like that.

特别 tèbié (副) especially; particularly 2 (形) special; particular; out of the ordinary:

这儿的西瓜特别甜。   The watermelon here is especially sweet.

多么(多)   duōme   (副) [used in an exclamatory or a compound sentence indicating high degree] how; what; however:

这些孩子多可爱呀！   How cute these children are!

极   jí   (副) extremely; exceedingly: HSK 3 new

他唱歌好极了！   tā chànggē hǎo jíle!   He sang very well!

几乎 jīhū (副) nearly; almost; practically: HSK 3 new

中国的大城市，我几乎都去过。   I have been to almost all of China's big cities.

4.3 范围副词：,   Fànwéi fùcí:,   Scope adverb:,
都   dōu (副) all; both: HSK 1 new

我们都看见那个人了。   We all saw that person.

一起 yīqǐ (副) Together; Together with   HSK 2 new

他们一起去机场了。   They went to the airport together.

一共 yīgòng   (副) altogether; in all; all told: HSK 3 new

这些药一共三百元。   These medicines total three hundred yuan.

只 zhǐ (副) only; merely: HSK 3 new

我只去过一次北京。   I have only been to Beijing once.

4.4 时间副词： Shíjiān fùcí: Time adverb:

正在   zhèngzài   (副) [to indicate an action in progress] in process of; in course of: HSK 2 new

我们正在看电视。   wǒmen zhèngzài kàn diànshì.   We are watching TV.

已经   yǐjīng   (副) already: HSK 2 new

他已经到学校了。   He has already arrived at school.

就   jiù   (副) at once; right away: HSK 2 new

他下个星期就回来了。　　　He will be back next week.

先　　　xiān　(副) earlier; before; first; in advance:　HSK 3　new

我先说几句。　　wǒ xiān shuō jǐ jù.　　Let me say a few words first.

才　Cái　only

他晚上十一点才下班。　　He only got off work at eleven o'clock in the evening.

一直　　　yīzhí　(副) straight:　　HSK 3　new

他的成绩一直很好。　　His performance has been very good.

总是　　　zǒng shì　　(副) always　HSK 3　new

她总是很忙。　　tā zǒng shì hěn máng.　　She is always very busy.

马上　　　mǎshàng　　(副) at once; straight away; right away; immediately:　HSK 3　new

请安静，节目马上开始。　　Please be quiet and the show will start right away.

4.5 语气副词： Yǔqì fùcí: Modal adverb:

也 yě (副) also; too as well: HSK 2 new

我也有一块这样的手表。 I also have a watch like this.

还 hái (副) 1 still; yet: HSK 2 new

他还没起床。 tā hái méi qǐchuáng. He hasn't got up yet.

真 zhēn (副) really; truly; indeed HSK 2 new

你的字写得真漂亮！ Your words are so beautiful!

终于 zhōngyú (副) at last; in the end HSK 3 new

考试终于结束了。 The exam is finally over.

其实 qí shí (副) actually; in fact; as a matter of fact HSK 3 new

这道题其实很容易。 This question is actually very easy.

当然　　　　dāngrán　　(形) of course; without doubt:　HSK 3 new

那样做当然不可以。　　　　　　Of course, you can't do that.

4.6　频率副词：　　　Pínlǜ fùcí: Frequency Adverb:

再　　　　zài　(副) again; once more　　HSK 2 new

欢迎再来！huānyíng zàilái!　　Welcome again!

又　　　　　yòu　(副) again and again　　　HSK 3 new

今天他又迟到了。　　　　　　He came late again today.

经常　　　　jīngcháng　　(副) frequently; constantly; regularly; often　HSK 3 new

最近他经常去爬山。　　　　　Recently he often went hiking.

4.7　更多副词：　　　More Adverbs:

故意　　　gùyì　(副) purposely; intentionally; deliberately:　HSK 4 new

他故意这么做的　　　　He did it on purpose

按时　　　ànshí　(副) on time; on schedule:　　　HSK 4 new

你要按时把书归还给图书馆。　　　You must return this book to the library on time

本来　　　běnlái　　　(副) originally　　HSK 4　new

本来他身体不好，现在很结实了　　　Originally he was in poor health but he is quite strong now.

不得不　　　bùdé bù　　　(副)have no choice (or option) but to; cannot but; have to:　HSK 4　new

时间不早了，我不得不走了　　　It's getting late. I'm afraid I have to leave now.

重新　chóngxīn　　(副) again; anew; afresh: -　　　HSK 4　new

扔了它，重新开始。　　　Throw it away and start again.

如果运动员抢跑，比赛就得重新开始。　　　If an athlete makes a false start, the race must be restarted.

孙子孙女让他重新变得充满活力。　　　His grandchildren have given him a new lease of life.

你上学期很懒，可是这学期我们会既往不咎，重新开始。　　　You were very lazy last term, but we'll start again with a clean sheet this term.

从来 　　　cónglái 　　　(副) always; all along: 　　　HSK 4 new

简从来不吃早饭。 　　　　　　Jane never eats breakfast.

胡说！他从来没有那样说过！ 　　　　　　Bullshit! He never said that!

他从来无法承认自己的错误。 　　　　　　He's never been able to admit to his mistakes.

我从来没有滑过雪——我对它从不感兴趣。 　　　uk I haven't been skiing - it's never really appealed.

为什么我讲了笑话，从来就没人笑呢？ 　　　Why does no one ever laugh at my jokes?

他真是游手好闲，从来没有干过一份正经的工作。 　　　He's a real deadbeat who's never had a proper job.

两国的关系从来没有像现在这么好过。 　　　Relations between the two countries have never been better.

大概 　　　dàgài 　　　(副) probably: 　　　HSK 4 new

她大概40岁刚出头。 　　　She's probably in her early forties.

大概有500人出席了会议。 　　　There were perhaps 500 people at the meeting.

这列火车大概在 10 点 30 分到站。　　　The train's approximate time of arrival is 10.30.

这项工作大概需时 3 周，费用为 1000 英镑左右。　　　The job will take approximately three weeks, and cost approximately £1,000.

你能告诉我要来的大概人数吗？　　　Could you give me a rough approximation of how many people will be coming?

修理费大概要 200 英镑。　　　The repair work will cost in the area of £200.

他们大概买得起一套大一点的公寓。　　　They can presumably afford to buy a bigger apartment.

到底　　　dàodǐ　　　(副) at last; finally; in the end　　HSK 4　new

你到底在干什么？　　　What the devil are you doing?

你认为自己到底在干什么？　　　What the deuce do you think you're doing?

他到底为什么那么做？　　　What the blazes did he do that for?

你到底什么意思？　　　What exactly do you mean?

我真不知道这么大惊小怪到底是怎么回事。　　　I really don't know what all the fuss is about.

那么到底发生了什么事呢？　　　So what actually happened?

归根到底就是钱的问题。　　　It all comes down to money in the end.

她对你这么不友好，到底什么原因？ What earthly reason can she have for being so horrible to you?

大约　　　dàyuē (副) approximately; about: 　　HSK 4　new

大约两个月前　　　about two months ago

我在这里住了大约两年了。 I've lived here for about two years.

会议大约在六点钟举行 The meeting took place at (round) about six o'clock

费用大约为 600 美元。 The approximate cost will be about $600.

50 美元是不是大约相当于 30 英镑？ Is $50 equivalent to about £30?

我们离家大约有一英里远。 We're about a mile from home.

她大约中等个子。 She's about average height (= neither short nor tall).

班上大约有一半是西班牙人，其余的则来自各个国家。 Roughly half (of) the class are Spanish and the others are a mixture of nationalities.

刚刚　　　gānggāng　(副) just; only; exactly　HSK 4　new

她刚刚大学毕业，人很聪明。 She's fresh out of college and very bright.

他刚刚当上爸爸。 He has just become a father.

果然　　　　guǒrán　　　(副) really; as expected; sure enough:　HSK 4　new

果然是他　guǒrán shì tā　　　It was him as expected

忽然　Hūrán(副) suddenly; all of a sudden　　HSK 4　new

忽然间他们就成了最好的朋友了。　　　　　Suddenly they were bezzie mates.

互相　　　　hùxiāng　　　(副) mutual; mutually:　　HSK 4　new

互相背对着的排屋　　　　　　uk back-to-back terraced houses

他们互相约定不透露任何细节。　　　　　They made a compact not to reveal any details.

如果你们俩都要撒谎，至少也要口径一致，不要互相矛盾！　　If you're both going to lie, at least stick to the same story and don't contradict each other!

我们是一帮碰了面就讨论问题、互相评论彼此作品的艺术家。　　We're a group of artists who meet to discuss ideas and criticize each other's work.

小组每个月都开一次会，这样成员之间就可以互相交流看法／观点。 Every month the group meets so its members can exchange their views/opinions (= have a discussion).

我们见面的时候可以互相留下对方的地址。 We can exchange addresses when we see each other.

他们开会前简短地互相致意。 They briskly exchanged greetings before starting the session.

他们在车站见面后互相拥抱。 They hugged each other when they met at the station.

我们见面时总是互相拥抱和亲吻。 We always exchange hugs and kisses when we meet.

今天早晨我们的邻居在互相破口大骂。 Our neighbours were yelling (obscenities) at each other this morning.

竟然　　　jìngrán　　　(副) unexpectedly; to one's surprise; actually: HSK 4 new

这样宏伟的建筑竟然只用十个月就完成了 It is amazing that it took merely ten months to complete such a magnificent building.

我们本以为会迟到 1 小时，结果竟然提前到了。 We had expected to arrive an hour late, but in the event we were early.

她竟然长那么高了，这让我很惊讶。 I was astonished by how much she'd grown.

她一反常态，竟然答应跟他一起去了。 In a moment of aberration, she agreed to go with him.

对不起，我迟到了。我一时糊涂，竟然忘了今天有会。 I'm sorry I'm late - I had a mental aberration and forgot we had a meeting today.

起初我对他并没有好感，可最后我竟然挺喜欢他的。 I didn't like him at first, but in the end I actually got quite fond of him.

不可思议的是，我们发现自己竟然住进了同一家旅馆。 Against all probability (= although it was extremely unlikely) we found ourselves in the same hotel.

竟然没有其他人去应聘这项工作，真让人惊诧。 It's amazing that no one else has applied for the job.

他们凭着花言巧语竟然混了进去。 Somehow they managed to blag their way in.

我觉得难以想象人们竟然还受着那样的虐待。 I find it hard to conceive (= it is too shocking to imagine) that people are still treated so badly.

极其 jíqí (副) most; extremely; exceedingly: HSK 4 new

这个地方自然风景极其优美。 This is an area of outstanding natural beauty.

他们结婚后极其幸福。 Since they got married, they've been in seventh heaven.

他是个极其有趣的人。 He's an absolute hoot.

沙漠中极其干旱，寸草不生。　　The desert is so arid that nothing can grow there.

到了 16 岁，晚上在家和父母呆在一起似乎是极其难受的事。　　When you're 16, an evening at home with your parents seems like a fate worse than death.

她对他的行为感到极其尴尬／忧虑／担忧。　　She felt acute embarrassment/anxiety/concern at his behaviour.

从哪方面说这都是笔极其糟糕的生意。　　It was a ghastly business all round.

这个话题引起了极其热烈的讨论。　　There was an extremely animated discussion on the subject.

犯人们被关押在条件极其恶劣的地方。　　Prisoners were kept in the most appalling conditions.

她的举止极其粗鲁。　　Her behaviour was nothing short of obnoxious.

究竟　Jiùjìng　　（副）[used in an interrogative sentence to make further inquiries] actually; exactly:　HSK 4　new

你究竟想说什么? nǐ jiūjìng xiǎng shuō shénme?　What on earth do you want to say?

你究竟去了哪里？　　Where the devil have you been?

你究竟对他做了什么？　　What ever have you done to him?

你究竟在胡说些什么？　　What on earth are you blathering on about?

你他妈那样做究竟是为了什么？ What the bloody hell did you do that for?

究竟是否能够实现自己的理想，她没有把握。 She doubts whether she'll ever be able to fulfil her ambition.

究竟发生了什么事？好好地告诉我吧。 Come on, what happened? Break it to me gently (= in a kind way).

我这就出去看看外面究竟在干什么。 I'll just go and find out what's going on outside.

你究竟是怎样设法让他同意的？ However did you manage to get him to agree to that?

这究竟是什么东西？我从没吃过这种东西。 What is this? I've never tasted anything like it.

你究竟是怎么想到那个主意的！ Wherever did you get that idea!

出国旅行这么多趟，他究竟是从哪儿弄到的钱？ Wherever does he get the money from to go on all these exotic journeys?

恐怕 kǒngpà （副）I'm afraid: HSK 4 new

"你知道我多大了吗？""恐怕我不知道。" Do you know how old I am? "I'm afraid you have the advantage of me there (= you know the answer but I do not)."

恐怕我对他作品的了解只是皮毛而已。 I'm afraid I have only a nodding acquaintance with his works.

这是你的房间——恐怕是太小了点儿。 This is your room - it's rather small, I'm afraid.

恐怕你完全误解了这个问题。 I'm afraid you've completely misunderstood the question.

"她赞赏我们的工作吗？""恐怕并非如此。" Was she impressed with our work? "I'm afraid not (= no)."

恐怕我别无选择，只有让你离开。 I'm afraid I have no alternative but to ask you to leave (= that is what I have to do).

恐怕我没注意听说了些什么。 I'm afraid I wasn't attending to what was being said.

我的节食计划过去一直进展顺利，但是最近恐怕有点儿退步。 My diet was going well, but I've been backsliding a little recently.

恐怕我对网球不是很感兴趣。 Tennis isn't really my bag, I'm afraid.

恐怕你给他忠告就好比对牛弹琴——他不会听的。 I'm afraid you're casting pearls before swine with your good advice - he won't listen.

恐怕那样的日子一去不复返了。 I'm afraid those days are gone and they'll never come again.

恐怕我的厨艺不怎么样！ My culinary skills are limited to boiling water (= I am not very good at cooking).

难道　　　　　nándào　　　　(副) [make an emphatic rhetorical question] HSK 4 new

你难道不喜欢她吗？　　　　　Don't you like her?

你难道不喜欢泡热水澡吗？　　　　Don't you just adore lying in a hot bath?

你难道不想明天把它完成吗？　　　Wouldn't you rather finish it tomorrow?

老在班里充当小丑，他难道不感到厌倦吗？　　Doesn't he get tired of playing the buffoon in class?

你们俩难道就不能言归于好吗？　　Can't you two just bury the hatchet?

你脑子里难道就没有点正经的笑话么？　　Can't you think of any clean jokes?

难道你不担心她会跟别人讲吗？　　Aren't you concerned (that) she might tell someone?

背叛了自己的同胞，难道他不感到愧疚吗？　　Didn't he feel guilty about betraying his fellow countrymen and women?

难道不是一切生物都具有某些权利吗？　　Don't all living creatures have certain rights?

难道你不讨厌每个周一又要回学校吗？　　Don't you hate going back to school on Mondays?

难道你不打算告诉我这个秘密？　　Aren't you going to let me in on (= tell me) the secret?

噢，真受不了！难道你想让我帮你干？   Oh, give me strength! Do you want me to do it for you?

你的吃相太难看了——你难道不会用刀叉吗？   Your table manners are awful - don't you know how to use a knife and fork?

怎么了？难道你连个玩笑都开不起？   What's the matter? Can't you take a joke?

谈论挣多少钱难道不庸俗吗？   Isn't it rather vulgar to talk about how much money you earn?

我们碰到这样的天气难道不够幸运吗？   Weren't we lucky with the weather?

偶尔 ǒu'ěr (副) once in a long while; occasionally: HSK 4 new

我偶尔打打网球。   I play the occasional game of tennis.

偶尔你该给自己放个假。   You have a duty to yourself to take a break once in a while.

下班后和周末时，我们偶尔会出去玩。   We go out once in a while after work and at the weekend.

你肯定会偶尔忘记别人的名字。   You're bound to forget people's names occasionally.

我偶尔还会想起她。   From time to time I still think of her.

我偶尔在城里见到他。   I see him occasionally in town.

他们偶尔会聚在一起喝杯啤酒。 Every now and again/then they'll have a beer together.

偶尔我也到高档餐厅犒劳自己一下。 Every so often I treat myself to a meal in an expensive restaurant.

偶尔少吃一顿饭对身体无害。 Missing a meal once in a while never did anyone any harm.

偶尔我喜欢看些通俗的动作片。 I like a lowbrow action movie once in a while.

夫妻之间偶尔发生口角是很平常的。 It's normal for couples to argue now and then.

我们偶尔聚在一起吃个午饭，但不如过去那么频繁了。 We meet up for lunch now and then, but not as often as we used to.

千万 qiān wàn (副) [used of exhortation or a friendly warning]: must HSK 4 new

千万要小心 qiān wàn yào xiǎoxīn Do be careful!

你千万别听他的 nǐ qiān wàn bié tīng tā de You must understand no circumstances believe what he says.; You must do not believe what he says in anyways.

行行好，千万别让她知道是我告诉你的！ For goodness' sake don't let her know I told you!

无论做什么，千万别告诉帕特里克。 Don't, whatever you do, tell Patrick (= you certainly should not tell him).

你千万不要在夜间不开车灯骑自行车。 You should never ride your bicycle without lights at night.

你千万不可违反规则。 You must not break the rules.

电器失火时，千万不要用水灭火。 Never use water to put out fires in electrical equipment.

移动家具时，千万别碰坏了油漆。 Make sure you don't mark the walls while you're moving the furniture around.

此人已是亡命之徒，可能还有枪，千万不要靠近。 This man is desperate and should not be approached since he may have a gun.

你知道他对饮食的那些坚持吧——在吃鱼时千万不要佐以红酒！ You know what he's like about food - thou shalt not serve red wine with fish.

我知道这很令人不快，但是千万不要因此而灰心。 I know it's frustrating, but don't let it get you down.

却　　què　（副）but; yet; however:　　HSK 4　new

我当时一定是傻了——我出去买东西却忘了带钱。 I must have had a brainstorm - I went shopping and forgot to take any money.

他是个典型的聪明却懒惰的孩子。 He's a classic example of a kid who's clever but lazy.

上学时我总觉得很吃力，而我妹妹却一路学得轻轻松松，成绩一直很优异。 While I struggled, my sister coasted through school with top grades.

她是法国人，但说话却是地道的英国腔。 She's French but she speaks with an impeccable English accent.

我以为你在努力工作，可你却一直在楼上睡觉！ There I was thinking you were hard at work and you were upstairs in bed all the while!

他喜欢第二辑，但我却觉得很糟糕。 He liked the second series and I thought it was a load of crap.

她这个年纪却有着那样的外表，我怀疑她做过整形手术。 I suspect she's had a nip and tuck to look like that at her age.

他表现得极为友善，但我却感觉很别扭。 His manner was perfectly amicable, but I felt uncomfortable.

她挑剔地看着他却没有说话。 She looked at him critically but said nothing.

我们好不容易到了家，却发现家里被盗了——这个现在就先甭提了。 When we finally got home, we found that we'd been burgled - but that's another story.

你期盼的事情一旦成真时，你却常常会感到并不如想象的那样令人兴奋。
When you really look forward to something it's often an anticlimax when it actually happens.

这家旅馆曾经非常好，可是近年来却失去了吸引力。 This used to be a marvellous hotel but it has lost its appeal in recent years.

上学时，我很擅长文科，但是理科却无可救药。 At school I was quite good at arts, but hopeless at science.

他们住了一个月却连句谢谢都没说就走了。这叫什么事啊！ They stayed for a month and left without even saying thank you! Well, I ask you!

她对人从来不怎么热情，但让我帮她写作业时，脸上却堆满了笑容。 She's never been very friendly, but she was all smiles when she asked me to help her with her homework.

她的名字就在我的嘴边却一时说不出来。 Her name is on the tip of my tongue.

城市璀璨的灯火吸引了许多年轻人，然而其中许多人却最终落得露宿街头。
For many young people, the bright lights of the city beckon, though a lot of them end up sleeping on the streets.

她在城市工作却住在乡村，可以尽享两种生活的好处。 She works in the city and lives in the country, so she gets the best of both worlds.

在车祸中他幸存了下来，但他的车却彻底报废了。 He survived the accident, but his car was damaged beyond repair.

确实　　　　　quèshí (副) really; indeed 2 (形) true; certain; reliable HSK 4　new

他独一无二，确实如此。　　　　　　　　He's one of a kind, he really is.

他女儿确实可爱漂亮。　　　　His daughter is a real cutie.

我不想离开大家，可我确实得走了。　　　　I don't want to break up the party but I have to go now.

我觉得他确实很怪，我真是一点儿也不明白他。　　　　I find him really odd - I can't figure him out at all.

"她对此确实很生气。""你能怪她吗？"　　　She's really furious about it. "Can you blame her (= I'm not surprised)?"

"这实在是个难题。""是呀，确实不容易。"　　　This is rather a difficult question. "Yes, it's certainly not easy."

从你到这儿以后你的英语确实有了进步。　　　There's been a definite improvement in your English since you came here.

她的新钢琴老师确实让她提高了。　　　Her new piano teacher has really brought her on.

他看上去确实好像在做什么坏事。　　　He certainly looked as if he was up to no good.

他确实得到了一个令人艳羡的位置。　　　He certainly earned his place in the sun.

没人说得清这个计划是否会奏效，但它确实是一个进步。　　　No one is sure whether this plan will work, but it's a step forward.

有段日子我们确实过得很艰难，但是现在一切都过去了。　　　We had a difficult time but it's all over now.

她确实是想对别人好，可是我和她碰面的时候，她真的不怎么样。　　She's meant to be really nice but she was anything but nice when I met her.

做这项工作，通晓数种语言确实是一种优势。　　Knowledge of languages is a real asset in this sort of work.

尼亚加拉瀑布确实是一处令人叹为观止的风景。　　Niagara Falls really is an awe-inspiring sight.

这段文章确实很难，不过你尽力翻译就可以了。　　It is a difficult passage, but just translate it as best you can.

她近来确实容光焕发。　　She has really blossomed recently.

他又失败了，但说句公道话，他确实尽力了。　　He failed again, but to give him his due, he did try hard.

到正午时，我们确实觉得热了。　　By midday, we were really feeling (= suffering from) the heat.

仍然　réngrán　（副）still; yet　　HSK 4　new

他们搬出去 3 个月了，这座房子仍然空着。　　Three months after they moved out, the house was still empty.

她虽然已经 43 岁了，但仍然很美，而且不知怎么地，总也不显老。　　She is beautiful and, at 43, somehow ageless.

到中场时，比分仍然是 4 平。　　　　The score at half-time was still four all.

假期里天天下雨——不过我们仍然玩得很开心。　　It rained every day of our holiday - but we had a good time all the same.

尽管出现了丑闻，这位领导人的反对者仍然未能赢得选举。　　Despite the scandal, the leader's opponents could not win at the ballot box.

嘻哈音乐现在仍然流行。　　　　Hip-hop is still big today.

我 17 岁了，可是乘公共汽车时仍然被视为儿童。　　I'm 17, but I'm still classed as a child when I travel by bus.

便宜的有机食品仍然很难买到。　　Cheap organic food is still difficult to come by.

我觉得我叔叔仍然把我看成是 4 岁的小孩。　　I think my uncle still conceives of me as a four-year-old.

她将近 86 岁了，每天早上仍然散步锻炼。　　She's nearly 86 and still takes a constitutional every morning.

他们已经争论了好几个小时，仍然没有得出一个结论。　　They had been debating for several hours without reaching a conclusion.

他仍然无法接受他们分手这一事实。　　He's still in denial about the break-up of his relationship.

这些问题的答案仍然是不得而知。　　The answers to these questions remain as elusive as ever.

但是对她来说，成功仍然不可企及。　　Success, however, remained elusive for her.

我仍然认为人性本善。　　I still believe that people are fundamentally good.

村里的老人仍然遵守当地的传统。　　The old people in the village still observe the local traditions.

这种病仍然困扰着医生们。　　The disease has continued to perplex doctors.

稍微　　shāowéi　　(副) a little; slightly:　　HSK 4 new

在外面稍微呆一会儿。　　a breath of air （a short period of time spent outside）

你就不能稍微变通一下吗？我只不过迟到了几分钟而已。　　Can't you bend the rules a little? I was only a few minutes late.

我们再稍微等一等，还不来的话我会给他们打电话的。　　We'll wait a little longer and then I'll phone them.

稍微有一点常识的人都会知道应该做什么。　　Anyone with a grain of common sense would have known what to do.

稍微犹豫了一下后，她开始讲话。　　After a slight hesitation, she began to speak.

那时候稍微软弱一点的人就可能会放弃。　　A lesser man (= a man who was not as strong or brave) might have given up at that point.

你可以把黄油稍微加热使其变软。 You can soften the butter by warming it gently.

甚至　shènzhì　　(副) even; (go) so far as to; so much so that:　HSK 4　new

今天甚至比昨天还热！　　Today is even hotter than yesterday!

政府甚至都不承认这个问题的存在。　　The government won't even acknowledge the existence of the problem.

我们的学生来自欧洲、亚洲甚至更远的地方。　　Our students come from Europe, Asia, and even further afield.

他甚至根本就没动笔。　　He hasn't even bothered to write.

我甚至连它在哪里都不知道。　　I don't even know where it is.

一些人信仰坚定，甚至为之坐牢也在所不惜。　　Some people hold their beliefs very strongly, even to the extent of being prepared to go to prison for them.

什么都提不起他的兴致，甚至连吃饭也不例外。　　Nothing - not even the prospect of dinner - could lift his spirits.

她自己提出了一个建议，甚至比我的还好。　　She topped my suggestion with an even better one of her own.

十分　　　shífēn　　(副) very; fully; utterly; extremely:　HSK 4　new

到了周末，市中心就变得十分热闹。 The city centre really comes alive at the weekend.

她十分热衷于养生保健。 She's a born-again health freak.

英国近年来人才外流现象十分严重。 Britain has suffered a huge brain drain in recent years.

大多数学生都十分贫困。 Most students are on/close to/below the breadline.

机场的安全检查变得十分严格。 Security checks have become really strict at the airport.

他对跑步十分着迷。 Running is a consuming passion with him.

桌子上吃的喝的应有尽有，十分丰盛。 The table held a veritable cornucopia of every kind of food or drink you could want.

这房间冬天十分温暖舒适。 This room is nice and cosy in the winter.

洛娜对她的男朋友十分着迷。 Lorna is completely crazy about her boyfriend.

她对自己的工作十分尽心尽力。 She's completely dedicated to her work.

露西对她的猫十分疼爱。 Lucy is devoted to her cats.

我小时候十分挑食。 I was a really faddy eater when I was young.

他吃东西十分挑剔。 He's terribly finicky about his food.

首先　　　　shǒuxiān　　（副）first; first of all　　　HSK 4　new

我首先得吃点东西。　　　　　I need to eat something first.

首先，我要感谢我的家人。　　　Above all, I'd like to thank my family.

首先，我要感谢我的父母。　　　First, I want to thank my parents.

首先，我想问你几个问题。　　　First (of all) (= before anything else), I'd like to ask you a few questions.

首先，我来介绍一下自己。　　　First off (= before anything else), let me introduce myself.

如果你想要出售房产，你首先必须证明你对它拥有所有权。　　　If you wish to sell the property, you will first have to prove your title to it.

首先仔细研究一下例题，然后试着做下一页的习题。　　　Study the examples first of all, then attempt the exercises on the next page.

顺便 shùnbiàn　　（副）by the way; incidentally; in passing:　　HSK 4　new

你去图书馆,顺便给我还这几本书　　　When you go to the library, please return these books for me if it doesn't give you too much inconvenience .

我用车顺便送你一下。　　　I'll give you a lift.

噢，顺便说一下，我叫祖莉。　　　Oh, by the way, my name's Julie.

我想需要讨论的问题我们都讨论了——顺便问一下，几点了？   I think we've discussed everything we need to - by the way, what time is it?

20 分钟后我在市中心还有个会，所以只好在路上顺便吃午饭了。   I've got a meeting downtown in 20 minutes so I'll have lunch on the hoof.

我在去超市的路上顺便接了孩子，一举两得。   I killed two birds with one stone and picked the kids up on the way to the supermarket.

我一个下午都在庭园里散步，顺便做些零活儿。   I spent the afternoon pottering around the garden doing a few odd jobs.

我回家的路上顺便去办公室收了一下邮件。   I stopped in at work on the way home to check my mail.

我回家的路上会顺便去一下商店，买些酒。   I'll stop off at the shops on my way home and get some wine.

挺　　tǐng　（副）very; rather; quite :　HSK 4　new

"这事挺费劲的！""不会吧！"   This is hard work! "No shit!"

那样挺好，谢谢你。   That'll do nicely, thank you.

他挺聪明的——嗯，绝对比他弟弟聪明。   He's fairly bright - well, certainly more so than his brother.

那看起来挺好的，不是么？   That looks good, doesn't it?

我挺喜欢你的耳环——你刚买的吗？ I like your earrings - are they a recent acquisition? (= Did you get them recently?)

起初我对他并没有好感，可最后我竟然挺喜欢他的。 I didn't like him at first, but in the end I actually got quite fond of him.

我们在地铁里迷了路，还真是挺惊险的。 We got lost on the Metro - it was quite an adventure.

他是个挺友好的家伙。 He's a friendly sort of a chap.

他提议如果我做饭，他就打扫卫生，这似乎挺公平合理的。 He offered to do all the cleaning if I did all the cooking, which seemed like a fair (= reasonable) deal.

他的玩笑挺好玩的，但有时候太过火了。 His jokes are funny, but sometimes he goes too far.

别再摆弄你的头发了，它看起来挺好的。 Stop fiddling about with your hair - it looks fine.

他们的新房子挺大的，但还是没有原来的房子大。 Their new house is largish, but it's not as big as their old one.

在辛苦工作整整一个星期后，放松一下挺好。 After toiling away at work all week, it's good to relax.

他人倒是挺好，只是不是我喜欢的那种类型。 He's a nice enough guy - he's just not my type.

站在外边挺冷的——进来暖和暖和吧。 It's cold standing out there - come into the warm.

往往 wǎngwǎng (副) often; frequently; more often than not　HSK 4 new

我往往白天睡觉，晚上学习。 I tend to sleep in/during the daytime and study at night.

老年人往往比年轻人怕冷。 Old people tend to feel the cold (= feel uncomfortable in cold temperatures) more than the young.

残疾人找工作往往很困难。 It is often very difficult for the disabled to find jobs.

男性往往比女性更具有攻击性。 Men tend to be more aggressive than women.

人生一世，往往起起落落，到头来还算公道。 The highs and lows of life tend to average out in the end.

随着年岁渐长，人们行事也往往一成不变起来。 As people get older, they often become set in their ways.

金钱往往是年轻夫妇关系紧张不和的起因。 Money is often a source of tension and disagreements in young married couples.

买房子往往会让年轻夫妇背上沉重的经济负担。 Buying a house often places a large financial burden on young couples.

男性成婚往往晚于女性。 Men tend to marry later than women.

青少年往往会有危险行为。 Teenagers often engage in risky behaviour.

如果你对青少年太严厉，他们往往会反叛。 If you are too strict with teenagers, they often rebel.

他 16 岁了，但往往看起来要小些。 He's 16, but he often seems (to be) younger.

游客往往花钱很大方。 Tourists are often big spenders (= they buy a lot of things).

西医往往治标不治本。 Western medicine tends to treat the symptoms and not the cause.

通常的看法认为女性比男性更情绪化，但依我的经验来看，事情往往不是这样。 Conventional/Received/Popular wisdom has it (= most people think) that women are more emotional than men, but in my experience it often isn't the case.

完全 wánquán （副）completely; fully; wholly; entirely; absolutely: (形) complete; whole: HSK 4 new

棒球赛使得观众们完全着了迷。 The baseball game completely enthralled the crowd.

我完全同意你的意见。 I agree with you completely.

他完全受自己情绪左右。　　He abandoned himself to his emotions.

我完全相信她的判断。　　I have absolute faith in her judgment.

那完全是一派胡言！　　That's absolute rubbish!

"不过这部电影棒极了。""完全同意！"　　It was an excellent film, though. "Absolutely!"

他完全沉迷于书中。　　He was completely absorbed in his book.

这种态度是完全无法接受的。　　This kind of attitude is simply not acceptable.

战争期间，这个城市几乎完全被夷为平地。　　The town was almost entirely destroyed during the war.

我完全赞成政府现在的做法。　　I thoroughly approve of what the government is doing.

酒后驾车完全是在自找麻烦。　　Drinking alcohol before driving is really asking for trouble.

我刚起床，还没完全醒呢。　　I've only just got up and I'm still half asleep (= not completely awake).

许多疾病是完全可以避免的。　　A number of illnesses are entirely avoidable.

他完全被她的美貌迷住了。　　He was completely beguiled by her beauty.

我一开起车来就完全变了一个人。　　I'm a different person when I'm behind the wheel.

要社会完全公平的理想只是幻想而已。 The ideal of a perfectly fair society is just make-believe.

最近我们完全没有丽扎的音信。 We haven't heard a dicky bird from (= spoken to or received a letter from) Riza recently.

机场完全被大雾封住了。 The airport was completely fogbound (= covered by fog).

谈判结果完全无法预测。 It is impossible to predict the outcome of the negotiations with any degree of certitude.

我得到这份工作完全是偶然。 I got this job completely by chance.

买新房子把我们完全掏空了。 Buying our new house has completely cleaned us out.

她的评论完全出乎人们的意料。 Her comments came out of left field.

我觉得他还没有完全接受妻子去世的事实。 I think he's still coming to terms with the death of his wife.

以她的资历，应该完全能胜任这份工作。 With her qualifications, she should fit the job perfectly.

也许 yěxǔ (副) perhaps; probably; maybe: HSK 4 new

也许早晨你应该早点起床。 [+ -ing verb] Maybe you should try getting up (= you should get up) earlier.

你也许有兴趣来看看我们在做什么。 You might like to come and see what we're doing out of interest (= because I think you might be interested).

我有一封信，也许你会感兴趣。 formal I have in my possession a letter which may be of interest to you.

如果我能存下足够的钱，明年我也许会来看你。 I might come and visit you next year, if I can save enough money.

现在雨也许已停了。 The rain might have stopped by now.

留着它，也许会有用。 Keep it, it might come in useful.

也许我们应该把这些想法写在纸上，免得忘记。 Perhaps we should commit these ideas to paper before we forget them.

你也许还会证明我是错的。 You might yet prove me wrong.

也许有些记忆很痛苦，你不得不把它们忘掉。 Perhaps there are some memories so bad that you have to blot them out.

如果提高教师的工资，也许会吸引更高水平的人才。 If teaching paid more it might attract people of (a) higher calibre.

这也许听起来很无情，可我并不在乎他是否无家可归。他又不和我住在一起！ It might sound callous, but I don't care if he's homeless. He's not living with me!

对于一个漫不经心的人来说，也许看上去一切正常。 To a casual observer, everything might appear normal.

也许明天他会把钱带回来，但我对此深表怀疑。 He may come back tomorrow with the money, but I very much doubt it.

她天真地相信他也许会来。 She fondly believed that he might come.

也许你会觉得，在他经历过这一切苦难后，他的子女们会对他多些同情。 You'd think his children would be more sympathetic towards him after all he's gone through (= the many bad things he has experienced).

事故的原因也许永远无法查清。 The cause of the accident may never be discovered.

也许有一天你们两个还会见面。 Maybe someday you'll both meet again.

抛弃安稳的工作进入充满未知的流行音乐界也许是个错误。Leaving a secure job for the twilight world of pop music may have been a mistake.

永远　　　　 yǒngyuǎn 　　(副) always ; forever; ever 　　 HSK 4 new

有些人永远不会满足！ Some people are never satisfied!

如果不再努力一些，你就永远不会成功。 You'll never be successful if you don't push yourself (= work) harder.

我永远也不会明白她为什么那么做。 I'll never comprehend why she did what she did.

我会永远记着你。 I'll always remember you.

他在花园里的身影永远留在我的记忆中。 My abiding memory is of him in the garden.

我永远也不会忘记第一次乘飞机的经历。 I'll never forget my first flight.

我们最后的谈话永远铭刻在我的记忆中。 That last conversation we had is engraved on my memory forever.

他将永远铭记那次事故。 figurative He will carry the memory of the accident with him (= will remember the accident) for ever.

要是你不给我一点提示，我永远也猜不到答案。 I'm never going to guess the answer if you don't give me a clue.

我的孩子们永远比我的事业重要。 My children will always come before my career.

别说了，懒鬼，你永远也不会有什么出息。 Come off it, deadbeat, you're never going to get anywhere.

如果没有我丈夫和家人的鼓励，我永远都不可能取得这样的成就。 I could never have achieved this without the encouragement of my husband and family.

他好像觉得我的钱永远花不完似的。 He seems to think that I have an endless supply of money.

你们俩永远也争吵不完！ Will you two never stop your eternal arguing!

但愿他的父母永远都不会发现。 God forbid (that) his parents should ever find out.

孩子们永远是活泼可爱的。 The children are always full of fun.

别借给他钱，你会永远要不回来的。 Don't lend him money - you'll never get it back.

别借给他钱，你会永远要不回来的。 Don't lend him money - you'll never get it back.

我觉得会计这工作他永远也做不好。 I can't see him ever making a go of accountancy.

人生的首要法则就是永远要表现得自信。 The first/most important rule in life is always to appear confident.

尤其 yóuqí (副) especially; particularly: HSK 4 new

在弗罗里达，今年冬天尤其寒冷。 The winter has been unusually cold for Florida.

这是困难的决定，尤其是对一个孩子来说。 It was a difficult decision, especially for a child.

低税率对于较为贫困的家庭尤其有利。 The lower tax rate is particularly advantageous to poorer families.

新的法律尤其适用于个体经营者。 The new laws have (a) particular application to the self-employed.

我们的研究重点是暗物质，尤其是如何利用天体物理学中来了解它。 Our research is focused on dark matter and in particular what we can learn about it using astrophysics.

我非常喜欢澳大利亚葡萄酒，尤其是白葡萄酒。 I love Australian wines, especially the white wines.

我对幼儿语言能力的发展尤其感兴趣。 I'm particularly interested in the linguistic development of young children.

我的狗有点儿胆小，尤其是在周围有其他狗的时候。 My dog is a little timid - especially around other dogs.

年幼孩子的父母常常罹患抑郁症，单身母亲尤其如此。 Parents of young children often become depressed, and this is especially true of single parents.

大型超市售价可以低于所有竞争对手，尤其是那些商业街上的小店铺。Big supermarkets can undercut all rivals, especially small family-owned shops.

这出戏很有意思，尤其是最后一幕令人捧腹。 It's a very amusing play with an uproarious final act.

只好　　　　　zhǐhǎo　　　　(副) have to:　　　　HSK 4　new

我只好把这项工作带回家完成。 I'll have to take this work home with me and finish it there.

如果这样不行，我们只好从头开始。 If this doesn't work we're back to square one.

如果雨再下大些的话，我们就只好回去了。 If the rain gets any worse we'll have to go back.

我演讲时忘了带稿，只好即兴发挥。 I'd forgotten the notes for my speech so I had to do it ad lib.

我找不到车站，只好问路。 I couldn't find the station, so I asked someone if they could direct me.

如果雨还下个不停，我们只好取消今晚的计划。 If the rain continues, we'll have to cancel tonight's plans.

他的发言很有说服力，我只好赞同。 His speech carried so much conviction that I had to agree with him.

她无家可归，只好让别人收养她的孩子。 She was homeless and had to put her child up for adoption (= ask for the child to be taken by someone else as their own).

我们走错了路，只好原路返回，直到找到正确的拐弯处。 We went the wrong way and had to backtrack till we got to the right turning.

我只好坐下喘口气。 I had to sit down and catch my breath.

我不知道答案，所以只好猜了。 I didn't know the answer, so I had to guess.

我们错过了公共汽车，所以只好步行。 We missed the bus and had to hoof it.

汽车又出毛病了，我们去海边的旅行只好作罢。 The car won't start. So much for our trip to the beach.

我把事情弄得一团糟，——只好重做了 I've made a muck of it - I'll have to do it again.

直接　　　zhíjiē　　　(形) direct; immediate:　　HSK 4　new

问题问得如此直接，让我有点儿吃惊。 I was a little taken aback at the directness of the question.

我直接从机场过来的。 I've come straight from the airport.

到河边后，我直接游了过去。 When I reached the river, I simply swam across.

我希望他进来前要敲门而不是直接闯入。 I wish he'd knock instead of just barging in.

她毫不留情地直接告诉我，我年纪太大，不适合这份工作。 She spoke with brutal honesty - I was too old for the job.

你为什么不当机立断，直接让他离开？ Why don't you take the bull by the horns and tell him to leave?

她决定直接管理这个项目。 She decided to take direct control of the project.

这路公共汽车直接去机场吗？ Does this bus go direct to the airport?

我打算直接向经理投诉。 I intended to go direct to the manager with my complaint.

日常饮食与心脏病有直接的关系。 There's a direct link between diet and heart disease.

她一回来就直接去了办公室。 On her return, she went straight to the office.

如果你需要什么，请直接同我联系吧。 Should you (= if you) ever need anything, please don't hesitate to contact me.

她拒绝直接加入争论的任何一方。 She refused to come down squarely on either side of the argument.

至少 zhìshǎo (副) at (the) least : HSK 4 new

你至少要等一个小时。 You'll have to wait at least an hour.

那个东西至少要花 100 美元。 It will cost at least $100.

他星期天至少要睡到上午 11 点才起床。 He never surfaces until at least 11.00 a.m. on a Sunday.

最好至少提前一周预订座位。 It's advisable to book seats at least a week in advance.

至少在这件事情上，他坚决站在了道义的一方。　　He was, in this matter at least, firmly on the side of the angels.

上班路上至少要花 1 个小时。　　It's at least an hour's commute to work.

他至少应该知道说句对不起。　　[+ to infinitive] He could at least have had the courtesy to say sorry.

至少他还干了件好事，把煤气关了。　　At least he had the good sense to turn the gas off.

至少有上千人在那里买票。　　There were no less than a thousand people there buying tickets.

你至少应该努力做出开心的样子！　　You might at least try to look like you're enjoying yourself!

每个问题至少有两个方面。　　There are at least two sides to every question.

我认为你至少应该提供帮助。　　I think the least you could do is offer to help.

逐渐　　zhújiàn　　(副) gradually:　　HSK 4 new

他感到自己逐渐失去了对事件的控制力。 He felt he was losing control of events.

随着课程逐渐变难，来上课的人也越来越少了。 As the course becomes more difficult, there's usually a corresponding drop in attendance.

我逐渐对这项计划成功的可能性产生了怀疑。 Doubts began to creep into my mind about the likely success of the project.

过去一年里，通货膨胀率逐渐上升，几乎达到了7%。 Over the last year, the rate of inflation has crept up to almost seven percent.

妻子死后，他对该项目的兴趣逐渐淡薄了。 His interest in the project declined after his wife died.

他能感觉到自己逐渐体力不支。 He could feel his strength ebbing (away).

热量逐渐消失在大气中。 The heat gradually dissipates into the atmosphere.

两国关系正逐渐恢复正常。 Relations between the two countries are gradually normalizing.

他非常害羞，但他在逐渐使她明白自己对她的感情。 He's very shy, but he's slowly working (his way/himself) up to letting her know what he feels about her.

5 连词 :　　　Liáncí:　Conjunction:

和　　hé　　(连) and :　　HSK 1　new

我和你。　　wǒ hé nǐ.　　Me and you.

因为 ... 所以 ...　　Yīnwèi… … suǒyǐ… …　Because ...　therefore ...　HSK 2 new

因为下雨，所以他没去踢足球。　　yīnwèi xià yǔ, suǒyǐ tā méi qù tī zúqiú.

He didn't play football because it was raining.

但是　dànshì　　(连) but; yet; still; nevertheless　HSK 2　new

他八十岁了，但是身体很好。　　tā bāshí suìle, dànshì shēntǐ hěn hǎo.　He is eighty years old, but he is in good health.

虽然 ... 但是(但) ...　　Although ... However ...

房子虽然旧了，但是很干净。　　　　　fángzi suīrán jiùle, dànshì hěn gānjìng.

The house is old but clean.

虽然有些小的地方让我不太满意，但总的来讲我还是很喜欢这份工作的。
There are a few small things that I don't like about my job, but by and large it's very enjoyable.

虽然这部小说在评论界赢得一片叫好之声，但并不畅销。　　Despite the critical acclaim, the novel did not sell well.

虽然他是一个很有竞争力的候选人，但他没有必胜的把握。Although he's a strong candidate, he's not a slam dunk.

那次活动虽然媒体很关注，但来参加的人却寥寥无几，与预期相差甚远。

After all that media attention, the whole event turned out to be a bit of a damp squib, with very few people attending.

虽然 ... 还是(还) ...　　　　　　Although ... But still ...

虽然很不情愿，他还是默许了这个计划。　　　Reluctantly, he acquiesced to/in the plans.

虽然我苦苦阻拦，他还是决定去。　　　He decided to go, although I begged him not to.

我虽然不会说他是才华横溢，可他还是能胜任工作的。　　I wouldn't say he was brilliant but he is competent at his job.

而且　　　　　　érqiě　(连) and also; moreover; in addition:　HSK 3　new

她会说汉语，而且说得很好。　　　　She speaks Chinese and speaks very well.

我不喜欢那个人，而且并不是我一个人这样觉得。　I don't like the man and I'm not alone in that (= other people agree).

我很冷，而且又饿又累。　　　　　I'm cold, and I'm also hungry and tired.

它太贵了，而且可能已过时了。　It's too expensive, and probably out-of-date at that.

他常去赌马而且下注很大。　　　He regularly goes to the races and bets heavily.

她觉得这些照片被滥用，而且败坏了她的名誉。　She felt that the photos were exploitative and cheapened her.

她是个身材小巧的孩子，不像她姐姐那样高大，而且还长着一双大脚。She was a small, dainty child, unlike her sister who was large and had big feet.

我不喜欢走路，而且讨厌露营。　　　I dislike walking and I hate camping.

她是个非常善良的人，而且十分慷慨。　She's a really sweet person and she's generous to a fault.

别的孩子总是取笑他，因为他胖而且还戴着眼镜。　The other children were always making fun of him because he was fat and wore glasses.

这座房子很漂亮，而且位置也非常好。　The house is beautiful. Furthermore, it's in a great location.

教师打孩子不仅在道德上是错误的，而且也是违法的。　For a teacher to hit a child is not just morally wrong but also illegal.

然后　ránhòu　　　(副) then; after that; afterwards　HSK 3　new

先吃饭，然后去看电影。　　　xiān chīfàn, ránhòu qù kàn diànyǐng.　Eat first, then go to the movies.

如果　　　　rúguǒ　　　(连) if; in case; in the event of:　HSK 3　new

如果大家都同意，就这样决定了。rúguǒ dàjiā dōu tóngyì, jiù zhèyàng juédìngle.　If everyone agrees, it is so decided.

一边　　　　yībiān　　　2 (副) [indicating two simultaneous actions] at the same time; simultaneously:

一边...一边...　　　yībiān... yībiān...　　[used before two verbs respectively to indicate simultaneous actions]　while...

他一边上网，一边听音乐。　　tā yībiān shàngwǎng, yībiān tīng yīnyuè.　　He listened to music while surfing the Internet.

或者（或） huòzhě （副）perhaps; maybe: 2 (连) or; either . . . or. . . : HSK 3 new

给我打电话或者发电子邮件都可以。 gěi wǒ dǎ diànhuà huòzhě fā diànzǐ yóujiàn dōu kěyǐ. Call me or email me.

还是 háishì（副）still; nevertheless; all the same: 3 (连) or: HSK 3 new

我们是打车还是坐地铁？ wǒmen shì dǎchē háishì zuò dìtiě? Are we taking a taxi or taking the subway?

并且 bìngqiě （连）and; besides; moreover; furthermore HSK 4 new

这本书很有趣，也很调侃，并且有时，不那么真诚。 The book is entertaining , meandering and at times disingenuous

不但 bùdàn （连）not only: (Usually used as 'not only ... (but) also') HSK 4 new

not only ... (but) also B2 不但...而且 used to say that two related things are true or happened, especially when this is surprising or shocking

他不但迟到了，而且还忘了带书。 Not only did he turn up late, he also forgot his books.

如果这个项目失败，不仅会影响到我们部门，而且还会对整个机构产生影响。

    If this project fails, it will affect not only our department, but also the whole organization.

她不但是画家而且是作家。 She's not only a painter but also a writer (= she is both).

我不但和她说了话，而且还得到了她的亲笔签名。 Not only did I speak to her, I even got her autograph!

不过   bùguò (连) only; merely; no more than: HSK 4 new

这本字典不过十美元。zhè běn zìdiǎn bùguò shí měiyuán. This dictionary costs no more than ten dollars.

不仅 bùjǐn 1 (连) not the only one: HSK 4 new

这不仅是我一个人的主张 zhè bùjīn shì wǒ yīgè rén de zhǔzhāng I'm not the only one who holds this view.

不仅 bùjǐn 2 not only:

不仅如此 bùjǐn rúcǐ not only that; nor is this all; moreover

大多数老师把他们的职业看作是一种使命，而不仅仅是一份工作。 Most teachers regard their profession as a vocation, not just a job.

一些饲养家禽的农民不仅养鸡，还养火鸡和鸭子。 Some poultry farmers keep turkeys and ducks as well as chickens.

对我来说，做生意不仅仅是个数字游戏。 To me, business is more than just a numbers game.

改善儿童保育设施对男女都会有好处，不仅仅是女性受益。 Improved childcare facilities would benefit both sexes, not just women.

而　　　ér　　(连) express coordination　　　　HSK 4　new

美丽而善良　　　měilì ér shànliáng　　　beautiful and kind-hearted

朴素而大方　　　púsù ér dàfāng　　　　simple and with good taste

而　　　ér　　2 [similar to "but" or "yet"] :

华而不实　huá'érbùshí　　　flashy without substance; meretricious[9]

这颜色艳而不俗　　　This colour is bright but not garish

而　　　ér　　3 [connect cause and effect; aim and means or action]:

因病而辞职　　　yīn bìng ér cízhí　　reslgn on health grounds.

为找工作而奔跑　　　hunting for a job

匆匆而来　　　cōngcōng ér lái　　come in a hurry

而　　　ér　　4 [indicate change from one state to another]

由远而近　　　yóu yuǎn ér jìn　　approach from afar

---

[9] meretricious　　　adjective　formal UK /ˌmer.ɪˈtrɪʃ.əs/ US /ˌmer.əˈtrɪʃ.əs/ 华而不实的，金玉其外的 seeming attractive but really false or of little value

由上而下　　yóu shàng ér xià　　from top to bottom

而后　　　　érhòu　　　　(副) after that; then

而今　　　　érjīn　　　　(名) now; at the present time

而且　　　　érqiě　　　　(连) and also; moreover; in addition:　HSK 3　new

他不但很懂画，而且自己画得也不错　　He knows a lot about painting, and he paints well himself.

不仅下了雪，而且下得很大　It not only snowed but also snowed heavily

而已 éryǐ　(助) that is all; nothing more:　HSK 6　new

不过开个玩笑而已　　　　　　　It's only a joke.

仅此而已　jǐncǐ'éryǐ　[no more] 只是这样罢了

如此而已　rúcǐ éryǐ　[that's what it all adds up to] 如此:像这样。而已:罢了。就是这样罢了

无疾而终　wújí'érzhōng　　[come to an eventual end] 没有病就死了,比喻事物未受外力干扰就自行消灭了

随遇而安　suíyù ér ān　[feel at home wherever one is;accept the circumstances with good will] 处在任何环境都能适应并感到满足

不一而足　bùyī'érzú　[too many to be enumerated;and so on] 不一一列举就足够了。形容很多

否则　　　　fǒuzé　　　　(连) otherwise; if not; or else:　　HSK 4　new

咱们现在就干，否则就晚了　　　　Let's get down to work at once, otherwise it'll be too late

尽管　jǐnguǎn　　　(连) though; even though; in spite of; despite　　　HSK 4 new

尽管有几个国家反对，决议还是通过了　　　　The resolution was passed in spite of opposition from a number of countries

既然　jìrán　(连) since; as; now that:　HSK 4　new

没咖啡了？既然如此，我就喝茶吧。　　　　There's no coffee left? In that case I'll have tea.

既然你已经了解了实际情况，你可以作出相应的选择了。　　　Now you know all the facts, you can make an informed choice.

既然就我一个人生活，我也就不常请人到家里做客。　　　Now that I live on my own, I don't entertain much.

既然圣诞节到了，我还是放弃节食吧。　　　Now that Christmas is here (= has begun), I might as well give up my diet.

既然无法改变这种状况，我只好试着去接受它。 I can't change the situation so I'm going to have to learn to live with it.

既然天气这么好，我们去外面吃饭／坐坐／走走好吗？ Since it's such a nice day, let's eat/sit/go outside.

你既然那么聪明，为什么不把它修好？ Why don't you fix it if you're so smart?

既然你已经来了，为什么不留下来喝杯茶呢？ Now that you're here, why don't you stop for some tea?

即使 jíshǐ (连) even; even if; even though: HSK 4 new

即使你当头儿，也不该摆架子 You shouldn't put on airs even if you were in charge.

即使如此，它依然不失为一部有力的小说。 Even so, it remains an effective novel .

即使是 6 岁大的孩子，晚上有时也可能会尿床。 Even a six-year-old can have an accident at night sometimes.

他不惜一切代价要得到她，即使这意味着放弃他自己所拥有的一切。 He wanted her at any cost, even if it meant giving up everything he had.

即使老了，他依然保留着那份童真。 Even as an old man he retained his boyish charm.

即使遭受酷刑，他也决不放弃自己的信念／信仰。　Even under torture, he refused to deny his beliefs/faith.

可是　　　　kěshì　　　　(连) but; yet; however:　HSK 4 new

你上学期很懒，可是这学期我们会既往不咎，重新开始。　You were very lazy last term, but we'll start again with a clean sheet this term.

他失去了 100 米跑的金牌，可是 400 米跑还有机会。He missed a medal in the 100 metres, but will get a second bite of the cherry in the 400 metres.

我昨晚打了电话，可是没人接。　I phoned last night but nobody answered.

我们力劝她不要辞职，可是没有用。　We tried to persuade her not to resign, but to no avail (= did not succeed).

她相貌平平，可是性格很可爱。　She's no oil painting but she's got an attractive personality.

张罗聚会她可是一把好手。　She's no slouch when it comes to organizing parties.

我一早上都在打电话，可是没打通。　I've been calling all morning but I can't get through.

她不想全日工作，可是不得不如此。　She doesn't want to work full-time, it's a case of having to.

我第一次见到他时并不喜欢他，可是现在已经改变了看法。　When I first met him I didn't like him but I've changed my mind.

他很会哄人，可是我不会信任他。 He's very charming but I wouldn't trust him.

我原打算去玩蹦极跳的，可是因为害怕放弃了。 I was going to go bungee jumping, but I chickened out.

朱迪向来不是很聪明，可是她很用功。 Judy has never been very clever, but she tries hard.

她和父亲的关系不好，可是和母亲的关系非常亲近。 Her relationship isn't good with her father, but she's very close to her mother.

那时她很老了，可是依然头脑清晰。 She was very old but still compos mentis.

她是一个身体发育良好的少年，可是智力水平只相当于 4 岁大的孩子。 She is a physically well-developed teenager with the mental level of a four-year-old.

然而　　　　rán'ér　　　　(连) yet; but; however　　HSK 4 new

城市璀璨的灯火吸引了许多年轻人，然而其中许多人却最终落得露宿街头。 For many young people, the bright lights of the city beckon, though a lot of them end up sleeping on the streets.

然而，可能还有其他我们不知道的原因。 There may, however, be other reasons that we don't know about.

她一直和老年人在一起工作，因此成为一名护士是自然而然的事。 She'd always worked with old people so becoming a nurse was a logical/natural progression.

危机逐日加深，然而政府似乎满足于无所事事。 Every day the crisis worsens and yet the government seems content to sit on its hands.

洗衣机淹水了，我的车出故障了，然而更糟的是我把自己锁在屋外了。The washing machine flooded, my car broke down, then to top it all I locked myself out of the house.

然而，他说的话至少有那么一点儿真实性。 And yet what he says contains at least a grain of (= a small amount of) truth.

无论　　　　wúlùn　　　　(连) no matter what, how, etc.; regardless of:　　　　HSK 4 new

无论是谁都不许无故缺席 Nobody should be absent without cause, no matter who he is.

无论如何　　　　(连) in any case; at any rate; whatever happens; at all events:

我们无论如何也得在今天做出决定 We've got to make a decision today, whatever happens .

无论天气好坏，我都要去。 I shall go regardless of the weather .

无论结果怎样，我都要努力。I will make great efforts no matter what the results will be

员工无论如何不能因为私事使用办公室电话。 Employees must on no account make personal phone calls from the office.

这些记录无论如何都不能改动。 These records must not on any account be changed.

我本来无论如何都不会错过你的聚会。 I wouldn't have missed your party for anything[10].

无论如何他都不应该动手打她。 He shouldn't have hit her, any way you slice it.

无论走到世界哪个地方，你都能看到这样或那样的汉堡快餐店。 Go anywhere in the world and you'll find some sort of hamburger restaurant.

无论做什么工作，都有利有弊，你都得承受。 You have to take the bad with the good in any career.

无论如何也难以相信人们会正儿八经把他称为艺术家。 By no stretch of the imagination could he be seriously described as an artist.

她干了那么多坏事，无论受到什么惩罚都是罪有应得。 After all the harm she's done, she deserves whatever she gets.

我也许下个月回家，但无论如何，我会在家过圣诞节的。 I might go home next month, but in any event, I'll be home for Christmas.

无论在哪里任何有理智的人都会对这种暴行义愤填膺。 Reasonable people everywhere will be outraged by this atrocity.

_____

[10] for anything (in the world)　　informal 无论如何 If you say that you would not do a particular thing for anything (in the world), it means that you certainly would not do it.

无论什么时候，都不要长时间晒太阳。　You should always limit your exposure to the sun.

无论如何，我必须走了——我都没意识到有多晚了！ Anyway, I must fly (= leave quickly) - I didn't realize how late it was!

因此　yīncǐ　(连) therefore; for this reason; consequently　HSK 4　new

语言是文化的载体，因此文化与外语教学有着不解之缘。　Language is the carrier of culture and soculture is closely related to foreign language teaching.

对此提议我们无法理解，因此更加难以信服。　The proposition is incomprehensible to us, and hence a fortiori we cannot be justified in believing it.

他好几个星期都不在国内，因此我把发生的事情全都告诉了他。　He'd been out of the country for weeks, so I clued him in on all that's been happening.

我们谁都没多少钱，因此就把我们所有的钱凑在一起吧。　None of us has much money so let's combine what we've got.

下周就要选举了，因此你到时必须在两者中作出选择。　The election is next week, so you'll have to come down on one side of the fence or the other by then.

那只狗很危险，因此他接到了把它人道毁灭的命令，但他拒绝服从。　He's been ordered to have the dog destroyed because it's dangerous, but he refuses to comply.

由于这些书极易受损，因此不宜搬动。　Because of their great delicacy, the books cannot be moved.

她上大学时热衷于参加体育运动，甚至因此还影响了学业。 She was very involved with sports at college, to the detriment of (= harming) her studies.

以前他从未对我说过谎，因此我没有理由怀疑他说的话。 He's never lied to me before, so I have no reason to doubt his word.

她离开都 6 个月了，可奇怪的是，她男朋友好像并没有因此不开心。 She's gone away for six months, but strangely/oddly/funnily enough (= surprisingly), her boyfriend doesn't seem too unhappy about it.

这个组织死守着自己的观点不变，因此常常受到批评。 The organization was often criticized for being too entrenched in its views.

我的膝盖仍然很疼，因此我向老师请假看能否不参加曲棍球训练。 I asked the teacher if I could be excused from (= allowed not to do) hockey practice as my knee still hurt.

他不喜欢我的决定，而我到现在还因此被他训斥。 He didn't like my decision, and I still get grief about it from him.

杰基病了，因此他们不得不改变计划。 Jackie's ill so they've had to change their plans.

这座房子有 4 个卧室，因此非常大。 The house has four bedrooms, so it's pretty big.

她是位有教养的女士，因此谈吐很得体。 She was an educated lady so she talked proper.

被告患有抑郁症，因此不能完全为她自己的行为负责。 The defendant was depressed and therefore not fully responsible for her own actions.

那是一个暖冬，因此我们省了不少电。 It was a warm winter, so we saved on electricity.

她一生为公众服务，因此获得奖励。 She was given the award for a lifetime of public service.

战争期间他的飞机被击落，他因此丧生。 He was killed during the war when his plane was shot down.

我要坐一整晚的车，因此我订了一个卧铺。 I'm travelling overnight so I've reserved a sleeper.

我的膝盖开始疼痛，因此我停下来不再跑了。 My knee started hurting so I stopped running.

警察说他的车在路上一直开得摇摇晃晃的，因此让他停了下来，给他做了个酒精测试。 The police said his car had been weaving all over the road, so they pulled him over and gave him a sobriety test.

我意识到我做的事情太多，因此我辞去了高尔夫球俱乐部的秘书一职。 I realized I'd been spreading myself too thin so I resigned as secretary of the golf club.

他坚决捍卫民权，因此赢得了声誉。 He gained a reputation as being a staunch defender/supporter of civil rights.

我们无法筹到资金，因此不得不放弃计划。 We were unable to get funding and therefore had to abandon the project.

他领悟力比较差，因此你可能得重复指导他好几遍。 He's a little slow on the uptake, so you may have to repeat the instructions a few times.

于是　　　yú shì　　　(连) thereupon; hence; consequently; as a result　　HSK 4　new

我在街上刚走出不远就想起来忘锁门了，于是马上转身跑回去。 I'd only gone a little way down the street when I remembered I hadn't locked the door, so I made/did a quick about-turn.

我的帽子戴歪了，于是我对着镜子正了正。　　My hat was askew so I adjusted it in the mirror.

安倒车时撞上了车库大门，于是她从此再也不开车了。　　Ann gave up driving when she backed the car into the garage door.

噪音开始干扰我们，于是我们就离开了。　　The noise was beginning to bother us, so we left.

那天天气晴好，于是他们决定逃学。　　It was a sunny day so they decided to bunk off school.

警察担心人群出现骚乱，于是骑马赶了过来。 The police feared that the crowd were becoming disorderly and so they moved in with horses.

我们发现走错了路，于是不得不原路返回。　　We realized we had taken the wrong road and had to double back.

他知道自己弄错了，于是便道了歉。 He knew he had been wrong, and duly apologized.

他发现自己丢了钱包，于是沿原路返回寻找。 When he realized he'd lost his wallet, he retraced his footsteps (= went back the way he had come).

他知道自己做错了事，于是羞愧地低下了头。 He knew he'd done something wrong and hung his head in shame.

当护士时见过各种可怕的事，于是你就对这些习以为常了。 You see all sorts of terrible things when you're a nurse so you become hardened to it.

我们看见下雨了，于是就匆忙躲进酒吧里。 We saw the rain and made a hasty retreat into the bar.

我感到不舒服，于是就回家了。 I felt ill so I went home.

所有人都想不出该再说些什么，于是会议陷入了沉默。 No one could think of anything more to say, and the meeting lapsed into silence.

我们想开车去海边，于是我们到海边过一个周末。 We wanted to drive up the coast, so we decided to make a weekend of it.

警方没能抓到杀害她儿子的凶手，于是她决定自己来解决此事。 When the police failed to catch her son's murderer, she decided to take matters into her own hands.

他们发现一只受伤的猫，于是精心照料直至它恢复健康。 They found an injured cat and carefully nursed it back to health (= until it was well again).

没有人想和我们同行，于是我们自己去了。 Nobody wanted to come with us, so we went by ourselves.

我被激怒，于是吵了起来。 I was provoked into the argument.

这些食物看起来很诱人，于是他决定每样菜都尝一点儿。 As the food looked so good, he decided to sample a little from each dish.

我在花园的深处找到一个幽静的地方，于是躺下来看书。 I found a sequestered spot in the park and lay down with my book.

面糊有点儿稀，于是我又加进了一些面粉。 The batter was a bit sloppy so I added some more flour.

我们累得连饭都做不动了，于是叫了外卖。 We were too tired to cook so we ordered takeaway.

一个老头正盯着她看，于是她朝他吐了吐舌头。 An old man was staring at her, so she stuck her tongue out at him.

我以前从不存钱，可现在年纪大了些，也更明智了，于是就能看出其中的意义。 I never used to save money but now I'm a little older and wiser I can see the point of it.

诺曼承认广告的措词冒犯性太强，于是便改掉了。 Norman agreed that the wording of the advertisement was unnecessarily offensive and it was changed.

只要 zhǐyào (连) so long as; provided: HSK 4 new

只要努力能掌握外语　zhǐyào nǔlì néng zhǎngwò wàiyǔ　so long as you work hard, you will be able to master a foreign language.

只要记住这点，就不会出问题。　As long as you remember this, there will be no problem.

我只要你们承认他的行为是无理取闹就行。　All I want is some acknowledgment that his behaviour is unreasonable.

我们应对问题的方式是只要出现就随时解决。　We deal with problems on an ad hoc basis (= as they happen).

我知道自己只要一开始看连续剧，就会马上上瘾，无法自拔。　I know that if I start watching a soap opera I immediately become hopelessly addicted.

多数情况下，只要摆上几盆花、几幅画，工作环境就能得到改善。Most working environments are improved by the addition of (= by adding) a few plants and pictures.

只要他幸福就行了——那是最重要的。　So long as he's happy - that's all that matters (= the most important thing).

我想我只要把家具全卖了就完事儿了。　I think I'll just sell all the furniture and have done with it.

只要有点吃的，就比没有强。　Any food would be better than nothing at all.

只要刷上一层漆，就会跟新的一样了。　A coat of paint and it will be as good as new.

你只要好好睡一晚上觉就会完全恢复了。 You just need a good night's sleep, and then you'll be right as rain again.

只要你尽力工作就行了。 Just do the job to the best of your ability.

只要再给他一点儿时间，他会同意我的观点的。 He'll come round to my point of view, given a bit of time.

只要告诉她我们不能——那她就没戏了。 Just tell her we can't - that'll cook her goose.

"乔说他想买辆摩托车。""只要我还有一口气就不准他买！" Joe says he's going to buy a motorbike. "Over my dead body!"

无论何时只要你认为合适，我们就会提供帮助。 We will provide help whenever you deem it appropriate.

只要他在足球场上发挥出水平，俱乐部就对他很满意。 As long as he does the business on the football field, the club is happy with him.

只要有机会我就会辞掉工作。 I'd give up work given half a chance.

只要看一眼伍迪•艾伦的脸就足以使我发笑。 Just seeing Woody Allen's face is enough to make me laugh.

只要你来，穿什么都没关系。 It doesn't matter what you wear - just as long as you come.

只要一提海鲜她就会觉得恶心。 The merest mention of seafood makes her feel sick.

只要有一点点批评他的意思就会让他警觉起来。　　The merest hint of criticism makes him defensive.

你可以想吃什么就吃什么，只要适量就好。　　You can eat whatever you want as long as it's in moderation.

这种水果只要去掉刺就可以吃了。　　The fruit can be eaten once the prickles have been removed.

任何时候只要项目出现问题，他都归咎到我个人身上。　　He held me personally responsible whenever anything went wrong in the project.

只要有争论，她就总是站在我父亲一边反对我。　　If ever there was any sort of argument, she'd always side with my father against me.

航空公司只要出一次乱子，就会给旅客留下持久的印象。　　A single snafu (= serious mistake) by an airline can leave a lasting impression on travelers.

我只要把我的东西收拾在一起，然后我们就可以离开。　　I'll just gather my stuff together, and then we can go.

只要你住在我家，就得听从我的规矩。　　While you're under my roof, you have to live by my rules.

他似乎认为我只要挥一挥魔杖，一切就都会解决了。　　He seems to think I can wave a magic wand and everything will be all right.

只要有可能，我就用蜂蜜来代替糖。　　Wherever possible I use honey instead of sugar.

有些人似乎认为只要他们希望疾病消失，疾病就会自行消失。　Some people seem to think if they wish the disease away, then it will go away.

6 介词：　jiècí:　Preposition:

在　zài　(介) [indicating the position of a person or thing]: at, on, in　HSK 1 new

我住在北京　wǒ zhù zài běijīng I live in Beijing

从　cóng　(介) [used to indicate the starting point] from; pass by:　HSK 2 new

她从中国回来了。　tā cóng zhōngguó huíláile.　She is back from China.

从…到…　cóng…dào…　from. . . to . . . :

从早到晚　cóng zǎo dào wǎn from morning till night.

从古到今   cóng gǔ dào jīn   from ancient times to the present.

从头到尾   cóngtóu dào wěi   from beginning to end

从东到西   cóng dōng dào xī   from east to west.

从上到下   cóng shàng dào xià from top to bottom; from the higher levels to grass roots

对   duì   (介) to; towards   HSK 2 new

他对我很好。   tā duì wǒ hěn hǎo. He treats me well.

比   bǐ   (介) [indicating difference in manner or degree by comparison] than HSK 2 new

我比他高。 wǒ bǐ tā gāo.   I am taller than him.

向   xiàng (介) to; towards   HSK 2 new

向左走。   xiàng zuǒ zǒu.   turn left.

他向我借钱，我没借给他。   He borrowed money from me and I didn't lend him.

我向她道歉，但是她不接受。   I offered her an apology, but she wouldn't accept it.

他向观众说了几句开场白。　　　　　He addressed a few introductory remarks to the audience.

我们向岸上游去。　　　　We swam ashore.

大风把船吹向陆地。　　　　Strong winds blew the ship ashore.

离　　　lí　　　(介) off; away; from; (away from, distance from)　　HSK 2　new

学校离我家很近。　　　xuéxiào lí wǒjiā hěn jìn.　The school is very close to my home.

跟　　gēn　　(连) and also　　　　HSK 3　new

你跟我们一起去吧。　　　nǐ gēn wǒmen yīqǐ qù ba. Let's go with us.

为　　wèi　　(介) [used together with 所 to indicate a passive structure]　HSK 3 new

不要为我担心。　　bùyào wèi wǒ dānxīn.　　Don't worry about me.

为了　　　　wèi le　　　(介) In order to, for (the purpose of)　　HSK 3　new

为了解决环境问题，人们想了很多办法。　　　　wèi liǎo jiějué huánjìng wèntí, rénmen xiǎngle hěnduō bànfǎ.　In order to solve environmental problems, people think a lot of ways.

除了　　　　chúle (介) except:　HSK 3　new

除了画画儿，她还喜欢跳舞。　　　　　　　In addition to painting, she also likes to dance.

把　　bǎ　　(介) [The usage of 把 often causes inversion with the object placed before the verb] Have sth Done; HSK 3　new

请把空调打开。　qǐng bǎ kòngtiáo dǎkāi.　Please turn on the air conditioner.

Version 2021 Notes:

Verb + Object (Things, Sth.[11])

喝水　hē shuǐ　　　Drink water

把[12] + Object (Things) + Verb　(Have Sth. done)

把水喝了　　bǎ shuǐ hēle Drink water

[11] Sth. Stands for Something.

[12] 把　　把 + sth. + Verb (Have sth. Done) [used to shift the object to the position before the verb, to indicate the disposal or the result of the disposal of the object (specific person or thing) by the verb] "把"用来把动词的宾语提到动词前面，表示动作动词对宾语(特定人或事物)的处置或处置结果。

打开书　　　dǎkāi shū　　Open the book

把书打开　　bǎ shū dǎkāi Open the book

吃饭　　　　　chīfàn　　　　　　Eat meal (eat food)

把饭吃了。bǎ fàn chīle.　　　Have the meal eaten.

吃完[13]饭　Chī wán fàn　　　Finish meal

把 + Object (Things) + Verb + Complementary (which shows the result of action)

把饭吃完　bǎ fàn chī wán　　Have the meal finished (Finish the meal!)

把饭吃干净　　　bǎ fàn chī gānjìng　　　Eat all cleanly.

Compare with another Passive words 被 (by)

Object (Things, Sth.) + 被[14] + （Sb.[15]）+ Verb　(Sth. Done by Sb.)

_____

[13] 完 wán （动）2 run out; use up: 3 finish: (here to show the result of action: to finish eating)

我们的汽油快用完了　　　　wǒmen de qìyóu kuài yòng wánliǎo　We are running out of petrol.

我要说的话完了　　wǒ yào shuō dehuà wánliǎo　That's all I wanted to say.

饭被他吃了。	fàn bèi tā chīle.	The meal was eaten by him.
饭被他吃完了。	Fàn bèi tā chī wánliǎo.	The meal was eaten all by him.
饭被他吃干净。	Fàn bèi tā chī gānjìng.	The meal was eaten cleanly by him.

More examples:

喝咖啡	Hē kāfēi	Drink coffee
把咖啡喝了。	bǎ kāfēi hēle.	Have the coffee drunk
咖啡被她喝了。	Kāfēi bèi tā hēle.	The coffee was drank by her

开车	Kāichē	Drive car
把车开走	bǎ chē kāi zǒu	Drive car away
他把车开走了。	tā bǎ chē kāi zǒule.	He drove the car away.
车被他开走了。	Chē bèi tā kāi zǒule.	The car was driven away by him.

---

[14]被 + Sb. + Verb (was Done by Somebody)   [used in a passive sentence to introduce the doer of the action The subject before the verb is the receiver of the action, and the verb is often followed by words indicating a completion or result. (The doer is often omitted in communication.)]用在被动句中，引进动作的施动者。前面的主语是动作的受动者。动词后边多有表示完成或结果的词语。(交际中施动者往往省略)

[15] Sb. Stands for Somebody

被　　bèi　（介）used before a notional verb to indicate that the subject is the receiver]:　HSK 3　new

鱼被小猫吃了。　yú bèi xiǎo māo chīle.　The fish was eaten by the kitten.

关于　guānyú　　（介）about; on; with regard to; concerning:　HSK 3　new

关于这段历史，我知道的很少。　　guānyú zhè duàn lìshǐ, wǒ zhīdào de hěn shǎo. I know very little about this history.

当　　dāng　（介）just at (a certain time or place)　HSK 4　new

当他苏醒过来的时候，发现自己已躺在医院病房里　When he came to, he found himself lying in a hospital ward

当我还是学生的时候，我并不需要很多睡眠。我常常一学就是一整夜！I didn't need much sleep when I was a student – I used to pull all-nighters[16] studying all the time!

当你发现某人肯定不会与你共患难的时候，就应该放弃这段友谊。因为他们只会在你需要帮助的时候让你失望。　　　　　　　When it becomes clear that someone is a fair-weather friend[17], you should walk away from the friendship. ~~They will only disappoint~~ you when you need them.

[16] Pull an all-nighter 开夜车表达

当我问及小陈她妈妈的时候，看得出来我触及到了她的痛处。　I could tell I'd touched a nerve[18] when I asked Chen about her mother.

连　　lián　　(介) even:　　HSK 4　new

连…也…　　　　　　even…also…

连…都…　　　　　　even…also…

大城市的书店，每天二十四小时营业，连周末也不休息。　Bookstores in big cities are open 24 hours a day, even on weekends.

这事连我妈都不知道，别说我了！　zhè shì lián wǒ mā dōu bù zhīdào, bié shuō wǒle! Even my mother is in the dark about it, to say nothing of me!

我连想都没有想过　　　Wǒ lián xiǎng dōu méiyǒu xiǎngguò　I didn't even give it a thought.

随着　　　　suízhe　　　(介) along with; in the wake of:　　　HSK 4　new

随着时间的推移 as time goes on; with the lapse (or passage) of time

---

[17] A fair-weather friend 酒肉朋友

[18] To touch a raw nerve 触及痛处

往　　wǎng (介) in the direction of; to; toward:　　HSK 4　new

往东走　　　　　　Go east

往左拐　　　　　　turn left

开往北京　　　　　Bound for Beijing

飞往沈阳　　　　　Fly to Shenyang

以　　yǐ　　(介) according to:　　HSK 4　new

以级别高低为序　yǐ jíbié gāodī wèi xù　　　in order of seniority

由　　yóu　　(介) because of; due to　　HSK 4　new

由于　yóuyú(介) due to; owing to; thanks to; as a result of　　　HSK 4　new

由于时间关系就谈到这里吧　yóuyú shíjiān guānxì jiù tán dào zhèlǐ ba　　　Since time is limited, I'll leave it at that.

与　　yǔ　　(介) with; to:　　　HSK 4　new

他与我同姓　　　tā yǔ wǒ tóngxìng　　　He is my namesake

与众不同　yǔzhòng-bùtóng　be out of the ordinary;be different from others] 跟众人不一样

时间与空间　　shíjiān yǔ kōngjiān　　　time and space

7 助动词 ：   zhùdòngcí: Auxiliary verb

会   Huì   (动) can; be able to: HSK 1 new

我会做饭   wǒ huì zuò fàn   I can cook

能   néng   (动) can; be able to: HSK 1 new

你什么时候能来? nǐ shénme shíhòu néng lái?   When can you come?

可以 kěyǐ (动) can; may: HSK 2 new

现在你可以走了。   xiànzài nǐ kěyǐ zǒule.   Now you can go.

要   yào   (动) want; desire: HSK 2 new

我要学游泳。   wǒ yào xué yóuyǒng.   I have to learn to swim.

可能 kěnéng (动) may

明天可能下雨。 míngtiān kěnéng xià yǔ. It may rain tomorrow.

应该 yīnggāi (动) should; Ought to HSK 3 new

我们应该在周末开个会。 wǒmen yīnggāi zài zhōumò kāi gè huì. We should have a meeting on the weekend.

愿意 Yuànyì (动) be willing; be ready; 2 wish; like ; want: HSK 3 new

你愿意和我结婚吗？ nǐ yuànyì hé wǒ jiéhūn ma? Would you like to marry me?

敢 gǎn (动) dare: HSK 3 new

你敢骑马吗？ nǐ gǎn qímǎ ma? Do you dare to ride a horse?

8 助词　zhùcí　Particle

8.1 结构助词：　jiégòu zhùcí:　Structural Particle

的　　de　　(助) [used after a pronoun] : show possession　　HSK 1 new

我的电脑　wǒ de diànnǎo　　my computer

书是哥哥的。　　shū shì gēgē de.　The book is my brother.

那个杯子是我的。　　nàgè bēizi shì wǒ de.　　That cup is mine.

这件衣服是最便宜的。　zhè jiàn yīfú shì zuì piányí de.　This dress is the cheapest.

我买了一些吃的。　　wǒ mǎile yīxiē chī de.　　I bought some food.

那边打电话的是我丈夫。　　nà biān dǎ diànhuà de shì wǒ zhàngfū. I was calling my husband over there.

得　　dé　　(助) used between a verb or an adjective and its complement to indicate result, possibility or degree]　　HSK 2　new

你做得对。nǐ zuò dé duì.　　　You are doing right.

地　　de　　(助) [used after an adjective, a noun or a phrase to form an adverbial adjunct before the verb] :　HSK 3　new

她高兴地笑了。　tā gāoxìng de xiàole.　　　She smiled happily.

Comparing "的 地 得"

的　　4 [used after a pronoun] : show possession　　　　HSK 1 new

你的，我的，大卫的…

地　　　　　Adjective + 地 + Verb　(Adjective to Adverb)
高兴　高兴地跑走了…

得　　1 (助)[used between a verb or an adjective and its complement to indicate result, possibility or degree]

得　　de　　1 (助)[used between a verb or an adjective and its complement to indicate result, possibility or degree]

Verb + 得 + complement
走得快　　zǒu de kuài　　walk fast.

唱得好　　chàng de hǎo　　sing well

办得到   bàn de dào   it can be done

拿得动   ná de dòng   can carry it.

雪下得大   xuě xià de dà   It snowed heavily.

拿得起来   ná de qǐ lái   can be picked up

擦得干净   cā de gānjìng can be wiped clean

Adjective + 得 + complement
病得厉害   bìng de lìhài   be very ill.

冷得打哆嗦lěng de dǎ duō suō   shiver with cold

Verb + 得 + complement Comparison of verb phrases
他打球打得比我好。   He plays ball better than me.

他打球比我打得好。   He plays ball better than me.

他球打得比我好。   He plays ball better than me.

Verb + 得 + complement
Verb complements; Resultative complements

看得见　　　kàn de jiàn　　　　Can see

看不见(Not 不看见）

买得到　　　mǎi de dào　　　Buy (and got it, Commercially available) (Lit.)
Can buy (Commercially available)

买到　bought (Buy and get it)

买不到 not 不买到

Adjective + 得 + complement
Intensifying complements

冷得很

冷极了

冷得不得了

Adjective + 得 + complement
Intensifying complements

美得很

美极了 marvelous

美得不得了 Incredibly beautiful

差得远 a far cry

忙得不可开交 be awfully (or terribly) busy

冻得全身颤 shiver all over with cold

得　de　2 (助) [used after certain verbs to indicate possibility] :

这种蘑菇吃得　　This kind of mushroom is edible

衬衣太短，穿不得了。　　　　The shirt is too short for me now.

这话可说不得。　We (You) mustn't say things like that.

8.2 语气助词：　　　　yǔqì zhùcí:　　Tone Particle

了　le　(助) to express a completed action　　HSK 1 new

她去医院了。　　tā qù yīyuànle.　She went to the hospital.

吗　ma　(助) [used at the end of a declarative sentence to transform it into a question]:　HSK 1 new

他是医生吗?　　　tā shì yīshēng ma? Is he a doctor?

呢　　ne　　(助) [used at the end of an interrogative sentence] :　　HSK 1 new

你在哪儿呢?　　nǐ zài nǎ'er ne?　　Where are you?

吧　　ba　　(助) 1 [used at the end of a sentence to indicate suggestion, requestor command]　HSK 2　new

快走吧!　　kuàizǒu ba! Let's go!

帮帮他吧　　Bāng bāng tā ba　　Let's give him a hand.

吧　　ba　　(助) 2 [used at the end of a sentence to indicate agreement or approval]:

好吧, 我答应你　hǎo ba, wǒ dāyìng nǐ　　OK, I promise.

吧　　ba　　(助) 3 [used at the end of a sentence to indicate doubt or conjecture] :

现在快十点了吧?　　xiànzài kuài shí diǎnle ba?　　It's almost ten o'clock now, right?

8.3 动态助词： dòngtài zhùcí: Aspect particle:

着 zhe (助) [indicating an action in progress] :   HSK 2 new

她笑着说："明天见." tā xiàozhe shuō:"Míngtiān jiàn."   She smiled and said: "See you tomorrow."

了 le (助) to express a completed action   HSK 1 new

她去医院了。   tā qù yīyuànle.   She went to the hospital.

我买了一本书。 wǒ mǎile yī běn shū.   I bought a book.

过 guò (助) [expressing the completion of action, or have experience in] had done …   HSK 2 new

我学过汉语。   wǒ xu.Guò hànyǔ. I have studied Chinese.

似的   shì de (助) [indicating similarity] :   HSK 5 new

像雪似的那么白 xiàng xuě shì dì nàme báias white as snow

他仿佛睡着了似的   tā fǎngfú shuìzhele shì deHe seems to be dozing off.

他乐得什么似的　tā lèdé shénme shì de　　He looks immensely happy .

嘛　　ma　　1 (助)　[used at the end of a sentence to show what precedes it is obvious]:　HSK 6　new

这样做就是不对嘛 !　　zhèyàng zuò jiùshì bùduì ma!　Of course it was acting improperly!

孩子总是孩子嘛! Háizi zǒng shì háizi ma!　Children are children!

嘛　　Ma　　2 [used within a sentence to mark a pause] :

你就不用亲自去了嘛　nǐ jiù bùyòng qīnzì qùle ma　　As for you, I don't think you have to go in person

啦　　la　　(助) [the representation of the combined sounds " le" and "a" , denoting exclamation, interrogation, etc.] :　HSK 6　new

他真来啦!　He has turned up, indeed!

这回我可亲眼看见她啦!　　This time I've actually seen her with my own eyes

左右 zuǒyòu　　　(助) about; more or less (名) the left and right sides (动) control; influence　HSK 6　new

五点钟左右　　　about five o'clock

两个月左右　　　　 two months or so

而已　éryǐ　(助) that is all; nothing more:　 HSK 6　new

不过开个玩笑而已　　bùguò kāi gè wánxiào éryǐ　　It's only a joke.

仅此而已　jǐncǐ'éryǐ　[no more] 只是这样罢了

如此而已　rúcǐ éryǐ　[that's what it all adds up to] 如此:像这样。而已:罢了。
就是这样罢了

9 叹词： tàn cí: Interjection:

喂 wèi (叹) [used in greeting or to attract attention] hello; hey: HSK 1 new

喂，你好。wèi, nǐ hǎo. Hello, How are you!

啊 a (叹) 1 a cry of surprise or amazement HSK 4 new

啊！这地方多美哇！ a! Zhè dìfāng duō měi wa! Oh, what a beautiful place!

啊，下雪了！ A, xià xuěle! Oh, it's snowing!

他的字写得多好啊。 Tā de zì xiě dé duō hǎo a.He has nice handwriting.

真漂亮啊！ zhēn piàoliang a! It's beautiful!

呀 ya (叹) [indicating surprise] ah; oh: HSK 4 new

呀,下雪了！ Oh, it's snowing!

唉　āi　（叹）(a sigh of sadness or regret）　　HSK 5　new

唉，太晚了　　āi, tài wǎnle　Oh, It's too late!

唉声叹气　Āishēngtànqì　　sigh in despair

哼　hēng　（叹）[expressing dissatisfaction or doubt] humph　HSK 6　new

哼, 你信他的!　　Humph! you believe him?

哦　Ó　（叹）[indicating doubt]:　HSK 6　new

哦! 会有这样的事?　　What! How could there be such things? or Really?

哦　Ó　（叹）[indicating understanding or realization]:

哦! 我懂了　　Oh! I see

哦! 我想起来了　Ah, I've got it

嗯　ń　（叹）[used for having words repeated when not heard]:　HSK 6
new

嗯　　ń　　1 (叹) [used for having words repeated when not heard]:

嗯，你说什么？　　what? what did you say?

嗯　　Ń　　2 (叹) [used to indicate surprise]:

嗯，怎么又不见了？ Hey! It's gone again.

嗯！你怎么还没去？　　What! You haven't started yet?

嘿　　hēi　　(叹) hey:　　HSK 6　new

嘿！快走吧！ Hey, hurry up!

嘿！下雪了　　Why, it's snowing!

唉哟　　　　āi yō　　　　(叹) Ouch! ; Hey!　HSK 6　new

哎哟，是你啊！　　Oh, it's you!

哎哟！都这么晚了。　　Ouch! It's all so late.

10 陈述句　Chénshùjù　Declarative Sentence

10.1 肯定句　kěndìng jù　Affirmative Sentence

明天星期六。　míngtiān xīngqíliù. Tomorrow is Saturday.

我认识他。　Wǒ rènshì tā.　I know him.

天气很好。　Tiānqì hěn hǎo.　The weather is great.

10.2 否定句：　Fǒudìng jù:　Negative Sentences:

不　bù　(副) [used to form a negative] no, not　HSK 1　new

他不在饭店。　tā bùzài fàndiàn.　He is not in the hotel.

没　méi　(副) not have; be without　HSK 1　new

她没去看电影。　tā méi qù kàn diànyǐng.　She did not go to the movies.

别　bié　(副) don't (used before verb)　HSK 2　new

别忘了带护照。　bié wàngle dài hùzhào.　Don't forget to bring your passport.

11 疑问词： yíwèn cí:　　Question words:

11.1 吗　ma　(助) [used at the end of a declarative sentence to transform it into a question]:　　HSK 1　new

这是你的桌子吗? zhè shì nǐ de zhuōzi ma? Is this your table?

呢　ne　(助) 1 用在反问句末,加强反问 [used at the end of an interrogative sentence]

我是老师，你呢？　　wǒ shì lǎoshī, nǐ ne?　　I am a teacher, what about you?

怎么办呢？ zěnme bàn ne?　　What is to be done?

她什么时候来呢？　　Tā shénme shíhòu lái ne?　　When will she be coming?

我喜欢他，你呢? Wǒ xǐhuān tā, nǐ ne?　　I like him. What about you? (or and you?)

我的大衣呢？　　Wǒ de dàyī ní?　　Where is my coat?

这件事谁不知道呢？　　Zhè jiàn shì shéi bù zhīdào ne? Who does not know this thing?

吧　ba　(助) 3 [used at the end of a sentence to indicate doubt or conjecture] :

你是中国人吧？　　nǐ shì zhōngguó rén ba? You're Chinese, right?

11.2 疑问代词　　yíwèn dàicí　　Interrogative pronouns

谁　shuí　(代) who:　HSK 1　new

那个人是谁?　　nàgè rén shì shéi?　who's that person?

哪　nǎ　(代) which; what:　HSK 1　new

这些杯子，你喜欢哪一个?　zhèxiē bēizi, nǐ xǐhuān nǎ yīgè? Which cup do you like?

哪儿 nǎ'er　(代) where; wherever:　HSK 1　new

你想去哪儿?　　nǐ xiǎng qù nǎ'er?　where do you want to go?

哪里 Nǎlǐ　(代) where; wherever:　HSK 1　new

你住在哪里?　　nǐ zhù zài nǎlǐ?　　where do you live?

什么 shénme　(代) what.　HSK 1　new

你爱吃什么水果?　　nǐ ài chī shénme shuǐguǒ?　　What fruit do you like to eat?

多少 duōshǎo　　(代) how many; how much:　　HSK 1　new

你们学校有多少学生？ nǐmen xuéxiào yǒu duōshǎo xuéshēng?　　How many students are there in your school?

几　 jǐ　　(代) how many (less than ten); few;　　HSK 1　new

你几岁了？ nǐ jǐ suìle?　how old are you?

现在几点？ Xiànzài jǐ diǎn?　　what time is it now?

你几点起床？　Nǐ jǐ diǎn qǐchuáng?　　What time do you get up?

今天星期几？　Jīntiān xīngqí jǐ?　What day is it today?

今天几月几号？　Jīntiān jǐ yuè jǐ hào?　　What date is it today?

怎么 Zěnme　　(代) [interrogative pronoun]　　HSK 1　new

你怎么了？ nǐ zěnmeliǎo?　　what happened to you?

怎么样　zěnme yàng (代) how [used as a predicative or complement]:　　HSK 1　new

这本书怎么样？　zhè běn shū zěnme yàng?How about this book?

为什么　　wèishéme　(代) why; why (or how) is it that　　HSK 2　new

他为什么没来？ tā wèishéme méi lái? Why didn't he come?

多　　duō　5 (副) [indicating degree or extent] :

从这儿到那儿多远？ cóng zhè'er dào nà'er duō yuǎn? How far is it from here to there?

多长时间　duō cháng shíjiān　(代) for how long; how long

多久　duōjiǔ(代) how long

这孩子多大了？ zhè háizi duōdàle? How old is this child?

11.3 正反疑问句　Zhèng fǎn yíwènjù　Affirmative-Negative questions

你喝不喝茶？ nǐ hē bù hē chá? Do you drink tea?

你决定了没有？ Nǐ juédìngle méiyǒu? Have you decided yet?

11.4 好吗　　Hǎo ma　Ok?

我们一起去，好吗？ wǒmen yīqǐ qù, hǎo ma? Let's go together, ok?

对吗 Duì ma　　right?

您要两张票，对吗？　　nín yào liǎng zhāng piào, duì ma?　　You want two tickets, right?

可以吗　　Kěyǐ ma　　Can?

中午吃面条儿，可以吗？　　zhōngwǔ chī miàntiáo er, kěyǐ ma?　　Eat noodles at noon, can you?

11.5 选择疑问句　　Xuǎnzé yíwènjù　　Alternative question

你喝茶还是喝咖啡？　　nǐ hē chá háishì hē kāfēi? Do you drink tea or coffee?

还是　háishì　　（副）still; nevertheless; all the same: 3（连）or:　　HSK 3 new

我们是打车还是坐地铁？　　wǒmen shì dǎchē háishì zuò dìtiě?　　Are we taking a taxi or taking the subway?

或者　huòzhě　　（副）perhaps; maybe: 2（连）or; either . . . or. . . :　　HSK 3 new

给我打电话或者发电子邮件都可以。　　gěi wǒ dǎ diànhuà huòzhě fā diànzǐ yóujiàn dōu kěyǐ.　　Call me or email me.

12 祈使句： Qíshǐjù: Imperative sentence:

12.1 请　Qǐng　please

请坐　qǐng zuò　Please sit

请进　qǐng jìn　Please enter

请喝茶　　qǐng hē chá　Please drink tea

12.2 别　bié　do not

别说话。　bié shuōhuà. Do not talk.

12.3 不要　Bùyào　Do not

不要吃太多。　bùyào chī tài duō.　Don't eat too much.

13 感叹句： Gǎntàn jù: Exclamatory sentence:

太　　Tài　　Too

太好了！　　tài hǎole!　　Great!

真　　zhēn　（副）really; truly; indeed　HSK 2 new

真好吃！　　zhēn hào chī!　　Really tasty!

多么(多)　　duōme　　（副）[used in an exclamatory or a compound sentence indicating high degree] how; what; however:　　HSK 3　new

他跑得多快啊！　　tā pǎo dé duō kuài a!　　How fast is he running!

极(了)　　jí　　（副）extremely; exceedingly:　　HSK 3　new

好极了！　　hǎo jíle!　　great!

14 特殊句型 Tèshū jù xíng   Special sentence pattern

14.1 "是" 字句 Shì zìjù   "是" sentence pattern

是   shì   1 (动) [used as the verb to be when the predicative is a noun] :

我是一个学生   wǒ shì yīgè xuéshēng   I am a student.

他是我的同学。   tā shì wǒ de tóngxué.   he is my classmate.

是   shì   2 [used for emphasis when the predicative is other than a noun] :

他是很努力的   tā shì hěn nǔlì de   He does work hard .

是   shì   3 [used to indicate existence] :

前边不远是一家旅馆   qiánbian bù yuǎn shì yījiā lǚguǎn   There is a hotel not far ahead

14.2 "有" 字句 Yǒu zìjù   "有" sentence pattern

有   yǒu   1 (动) have; possess

有   yǒu   2 there is; exist:

一年有十二个月。   yī nián yǒu shí'èr gè yuè. There are twelve months in a year.

这里边什么东西都没有 zhè lǐbian shénme dōngxī dū méiyǒu There is nothing whatever in here.

14.3 是 ... 的 字句型　　shì zìjù　　是 plus stative verb for emphasis

强调时间　　qiángdiào shíjiān　　Emphasize time

我是昨天来的。　wǒ shì zuótiān lái de.　I came yesterday.

强调地点　　Qiángdiào dìdiǎn　　Emphasis on location

这是在火车站买的。　zhè shì zài huǒchē zhàn mǎi de. This was bought at the train station.

强调方式　　Qiángdiào fāngshì　　Emphasis

他是坐飞机来的　tā shì zuò fēijī lái de　He is coming by plane

14.4 比较句　bǐjiào jù　Comparative sentence

比　　bǐ　　(介) [indicating difference in manner or degree by comparison] than HSK 2 new

今天比昨天冷。　jīntiān bǐ zuótiān lěng.　Today is colder than yesterday.

和 (跟）… …一样　　Hé (gēn)… …yīyàng　　Same as (with)

他和我一样高。　tā hé wǒ yīyàng gāo.　He is as tall as me.

没有　Méiyǒu　　No

上海没有北京冷。　shànghǎi méiyǒu běijīng lěng.　Shanghai is not cold than Beijing.

没有……那么（这么）　　　　Méiyǒu… …nàme (zhème)　　No... then (so)

上海没有北京那么冷。　shànghǎi méiyǒu běijīng nàme lěng.　Shanghai is not as cold as Beijing.

14.5 "把"字句 "Bǎ" zìjù Passive Sentence using "把" Have Sth done

我把衣服洗了。　wǒ bǎ yīfú xǐle.　I washed my clothes. (I have clothes washed)

14.6 被 被动句　Bèidòng jù　Passive sentence using "被" Sth done by somebody

行李箱被司机拿走了。　xínglǐ xiāng bèi sījī ná zǒule.　The suitcase was taken away by the driver.

14.7 连动句　Lián dòng jù　Sentences with verbal constructions in series

他每天骑车上班。　　　tā měitiān qí chē shàngbān.　He rides to work every day.

14.8 存现句　Cún xiàn jù　Existential sentence

桌子上放着一本书。　zhuōzi shàng fàngzhe yī běn shū.　There is a book on the table.

有　　yǒu　2 there is; exist:

一年有十二个月。　　yī nián yǒu shí'èr gè yuè. There are twelve months in a year.

这里边什么东西都没有 zhè lǐbian shénme dōngxī dū méiyǒu There is nothing whatever in here.

Somewhere (Place A) HAS Something

桌上有一本书。　zhuō shàng yǒuyī běn shū.　　There is a book on the table.

Something AT Somewhere.

有一本书在桌上。　　Yǒuyī běn shū zài zhuō shàng. There is a book on the table.

家里有人。　　jiā li yǒurén.　　Someone at home.

有人在家里。　Yǒurén zài jiālǐ.　Someone at home.

里面有苹果。　Lǐmiàn yǒu píngguǒ.　There are apples inside.

苹果在里面。　Píngguǒ zài lǐmiàn.　　There are apples inside.

14.9 兼语句 Jiān yǔjù Concurrent statement

小王叫我去他家玩儿。 xiǎo wáng jiào wǒ qù tā jiā wán er. Xiao Wang told me to go to his house to play.

15 动作的状态 Tense of action

15.1 用 "在... 呢" 表示动作正在进行。 Use "In..." to indicate that the action is in progress.

他们在吃饭呢。 Tāmen zài chīfàn ne. They are eating

正在(在) zhèngzài (副) [to indicate an action in progress] in process of; in course of: HSK 2 new.

15.2 用 "正在 " 表示动作正在进行。 Use "being" to indicate that the action is in progress.

他们正在打篮球。 Tāmen zhèngzài dǎ lánqiú. They are playing basketball.

正在 zhèngzài (副) [to indicate an action in progress] in process of; in course of: HSK 2 new

15.3 用 "了 " "过 "表示动作已经完成。 Use "has" and "over" to indicate that the action has been completed.

了 le (助) to express a completed action HSK 1 new

她去医院了。 tā qù yīyuànle. She went to the hospital. V2020

他买了一公斤苹果。 Tā mǎile yī gōngjīn píngguǒ. He bought a kilogram of apple.

过 guò (助) [expressing the completion of action] HSK 2 new

我学过汉语。 wǒ xu.Guò hànyǔ. I have studied Chinese. V2020

我看过这个电影。　　　　Wǒ kànguò zhège diànyǐng.　　I have seen this movie.

15.4 用 "要 ... 了 " 表示动作(变化)将要发生。　　Yòng"yào...
...le" biǎoshì dòngzuò (biànhuà) jiāngyào fāshēng. Use "To..." to
indicate that an action (change) is about to occur.

火车要开了。　　　　Huǒchē yào kāile.　The train is going to open.

15.5 用 "着 " 表示动作(状态)的持续。　　　　Yòng"zhe" biǎoshì
dòngzuò (zhuàngtài) de chíxù.　　　Use "to" to indicate the
duration of the action (state).

着　　zhe　　(助) [indicating an action in progress] :　　HSK 2 new

外面下着雨。　　Wàimiàn xiàzhe yǔ.　　It was raining outside.

16 动词的重叠 Reduplication of verbs

你去问问他。　　　nǐ qù wèn wèn tā.　Go ask him.

让我想一想。　　　Ràng wǒ xiǎng yī xiǎng.　Let me think about it.

We offer more…

Design Your Own Program, Customize the Courses using Your Own LOGO

- Professional book design using Microsoft Words, with Content, footnotes to explain vocab, grammar etc.

- Convert your school teaching material into the Professional one!

- Convert your school teaching material into PDF file with your own LOGO as watermark

- Protect your PDF files using our know-how skill to prevent copy!

- Save your time on teaching!

- Engage and encourage your students

- Using Microsoft Words file for classroom presentation or Online teaching in a creative way you may never heard

-Convert Microsoft Words document into Video (with background music or narrations)

-Create PPT file for classroom presentation or Online teaching

-Customize the courses using your own LOGO.,

-Create the Promotion Video like a Pro!

-Publish and sell your books (eBook or Paperback book) in Amazon, Google Play Books, and Apple Books as Pro. Your Name will be Author or Co Author

-Publish and sell your Video course on Udemy

-Create online Quiz and auto-grading, save your time in teaching and assessing

-Share Quiz with your students and engaging

-Share your works through social media platform

-Give and control access for your own students

-Easy to integrate the online system with your school system or your social media platform

-Keep using and updating!

-Worry free, hand free, just enjoy your life... AI and automation will help your teaching!

-Build up your own ecommerce Website

-Franchising opportunity

-Online Teaching Tips and Skills

-Social Media Marketing

-online quiz

-Systematic organize your materials for online teaching and sharing.

We welcome Teachers to join our group!

We welcome teacher to join our Facebook group: Chinese Course book, Video Course Design, Research and sharing 中文海外教材教程研究.

Edeo (Educational Video Online Courses) is one of the pioneering online Courses Creators. We provide Contents and Solutions, online, offline, in Classroom presentation or online lessons, group assignments or personal learning management. We welcome Teachers to join our group and marketing networks (more than 1 million users in our networks and social media, YouTube, Udemy, Amazon, iBook, Teachlr, Google Books, Rakuten Kobo etc.) for:

- Developing and publishing books, teaching materials

- Creating and marketing online Video

- Hosting online live courses

https://www.facebook.com/groups/2896012267340830/